W9-BTK-918

THE TEACHING TENNIS PRO

WRITE FOR OUR FREE CATALOG

If there is a Pinnacle Book you want—and you cannot find it locally—it is available from us simply by sending the title and price plus 50¢ per order and 10¢ per copy to cover mailing and handling costs to:

Pinnacle Book Services
P.O. Box 690
New York, N.Y. 10019

Please allow 4 weeks for delivery. New York State and California residents add applicable sales tax.

———— Check here if you want to receive our catalog regularly.

THE
TEACHING
TENNIS
PRO

DON J. LEARY

Introduction by Jack Kramer

PINNACLE BOOKS   LOS ANGELES

THE TEACHING TENNIS PRO

Copyright © 1979 by Don J. Leary
Art copyright © 1977, 1978, 1979 by Los Angeles Times Syndicate

Text art by Roger Vega

All rights reserved, including the right to reproduce this book
or portions thereof in any form.

An original Pinnacle Books edition, published for
the first time anywhere.

First printing, May 1979

ISBN: 0-523-40574-X

Printed in the United States of America

PINNACLE BOOKS, INC.
2029 Century Park East
Los Angeles, California 90067

CONTENTS

INTRODUCTION
by Jack Kramer

My association with Don Leary dates back some twenty-five years, to a time when Don would ball-boy Davis Cup team matches and exhibition tournaments held at the Balboa Bay Club, Newport Beach, California. He was twelve years old, a Southern California junior player, serving a true tennis apprenticeship/assistantship under Charles S. Eaton, his mentor pro and then head tennis professional at the Balboa Bay Club.

At that time Don was what we know today as the "club ball machine." When he wasn't playing tournaments, he would be washing courts, valeting the men's room, working in the pro shop, and generally polishing up the whole club—simply for club playing privileges. Those playing privileges were defined generally as hitting by the hour with "C" and "D" tennis players who had just taken a lesson and needed practice. In addition, he would act as a fill-in in social

1

matches with the likes of myself, when my wife and I would visit the Bay Club with our friends.

Don has been, as the old expression goes, "from the boot straps on up" in tennis. He started when he was seven years old—ball-boying, playing tournaments, sleeping in the pro shop and watch-dogging it, and ultimately becoming the formal assistant pro. He would give lessons at the Balboa Bay Club during summers and vacations when he wasn't attending high school and college. You could always find him hanging around the head tennis professionals in clubs, from Pebble Beach to San Diego's La Jolla Beach and Tennis Club. He was destined to become a "Teaching Tennis Professional," the very thing he wanted most.

It's no wonder that he now has one of the most brilliant teaching pro careers in the nation, or internationally, for that matter. To date, he has been the head resident professional at the Pebble Beach Tennis Club, the Tennis Club of Palm Springs, the La Jolla Beach and Tennis Club, the Seattle Tennis Club—and presently, the scene of his tennis roots, the Balboa Bay Club. These five clubs are among the crème de la crème of the world.

Regardless of success, Don has always been totally involved in his teaching profession and is known for the long daily hours—6 A.M. to 6 P.M.—that he logs on the teaching court. He has done this for seventeen years as a head professional, and that represents thousands of lessons and pupils—a world of experience.

He has collected one of the finest and largest tennis libraries in the world, some 350 volumes—literally almost every word that has ever been put down about tennis in book form. He has been compiling this library

2

from age fifteen. Mr. Harry Levinson, a rare-book collector/dealer in Beverly Hills, assisted Don. Levinson would buy up whole European estate libraries and subsequently sell the finest tennis volumes to Don.

Administratively speaking, Don has always been innovative, enthusiastic and a leader in the United States Professional Tennis Association, the national association that certifies teaching professionals through written, verbal, and court examinations. Don was the founder, Regional Vice-President and ultimately President of the Pacific Northwest Division, including British Columbia, Canada, while he was at the Seattle Tennis Club. He has been a member of the U.S.P.T.A. for fifteen years.

Don has always had an academic interest in tennis. He has always been a writer and has had published numerous newspaper and magazine articles, both in the U.S. and Europe, encompassing the total perspective of the tennis world.

It is not surprising that in 1975 the *Los Angeles Times* syndicate contracted Don to do an instructional tennis feature column called, appropriately, "The Teaching Pro." It appears three times weekly in newspapers all over the world, incorporating an audience of better than 30 million readers from many locations including Japan, Singapore, Canada, and Indonesia, not to mention the U.S. As Don says, "It's wonderful to give a lesson to millions of people rather than just one at a time on the teaching court. It's rewarding to put down, in line drawings and catching text, mental word-pictures that people can relate to easily, instead of trying to decipher the teaching pro's way of articulation."

This last point is exactly what Don's book is about. As he says, "The simplest things in life are most successful." He has provided an instructional approach that encompasses all the strokes in the game, covers tactics, strategy, miscellaneous items such as conditioning and equipment, and even includes a glossary.

The presentation of each panel in this book comes straight from a teaching pro's world. These helpful hints have been tested through years of experience, and are presented here clearly, briefly, and systematically, to make the game of tennis easier for any student.

This book should interest almost every tennis player. There is something for everyone—beginner, intermediate, or advanced. High school and college coaches and pupils can use this book to advantage, not to mention the millions of park, recreational, and club players.

This book, the first of several volumes, is a compilation of material from Don's "Teaching Pro" column. Every player should try the tips, mental images, and graphics that form Don's truly unique approach to instructional tennis writing.

Jack Kramer

Jack Kramer, author of *How To Play Your Best Tennis All the Time*, is known as the father of modern tennis and is often credited with being the originator of the "big game," known as the serve-and-volley attacking game.

In 1946–47, Jack Kramer was the United States champion. He won Wimbledon twice and was the front runner on the world championship U.S. Davis Cup team. Subsequently, he won numerous major international titles in both singles and doubles before turning professional in 1948. As a professional, he was the number-one player in the world. Today, in 1979, Kramer is still revered as the patron saint of modern day tennis. He has served for fifteen years as the expert analyst/commentator for the games universally known as one Premier Championship—Wimbledon—viewed from all over the world by the most knowledgeable tennis aficionados. Moreover, for twenty years he was the master commentator on network television for the Forest Hills Championships.

Jack Kramer still attends most major championship events in one or another of his various roles as promoter, administrator, and *éminence grise* of the pro circuit.

HOW TO USE THIS BOOK

This book is designed to teach you how to be your own tennis pro—in other words, how to teach yourself, your children, or your friends how to play and enjoy the game of tennis, using step-by-step, how-to-do-it art and text.

Learning the game of tennis is not an easy undertaking; however, once learned properly, it is the game of a lifetime.

I've always felt that instruction is valuable in any sport, but in tennis, golf, and skiing I feel it's an absolute necessity. Success in these sports depends greatly on style, rhythm, grace, coordination, timing, concentration, proper practice, and conditioning. And the mental approach to the sport incorporating strategy, tactics, control, temperament, and court presence is equally important.

Tennis, even more than golf and skiing, requires all

the above skills. To play the game well, each one of the above factors must be strongly developed.

The three most common questions about learning tennis are: What's the easiest way of going about it? Which one of the many aspects of tennis should I study first? How can I do it quickly and have fun doing it?

Naturally, being a teaching pro, I think the best way is to find a certified instructor and pursue the game under his or her tutelage. But this book is for the many millions of readers all over the world who cannot afford lessons, or who don't have access to a pro. It has been written in such a way that it makes learning easy *without* live instruction. It can be used by beginning, intermediate, and advanced players from ages eight to eighty, by tennis teachers, high school and college coaches, and individual players.

As a head tennis professional for seventeen years, I know the stumbling blocks, bottlenecks, and hazards often confronted by aspiring tennis players. Learning tennis can be extremely arduous; in this book I have attempted to take the difficulties of the game and make them easy for you.

When I give a tennis lesson, it is divided into four areas:

1. Diagnosing the problem.
2. Articulating the problem to the students; in other words, telling them what is wrong.
3. Showing them how to do it correctly.
4. Fortifying the correction with word-pictures, mental graphics, verbal tricks, and hints that the students can use in practice.

The mental word-pictures are the secrets to this book

7

and to the success of your game. A good teaching professional is adept at making the student understand exactly where he or she is going wrong, and exactly what to do about it. How does the pro do it? Through mental word-pictures. The better the pro, the more word-pictures he has in his verbal repertoire. He can communicate well, and solve problems easily.

Let's define what I mean by word-pictures, since in this book you will find almost 200 of them. Look at any page and you will see an illustration, with a headline and with smaller descriptive copy. The purpose of each picture is to convey an instructional point to you, the reader. Hopefully, you will absorb the point easily, aided by the descriptive word-picture.

For instance, if I'm trying to describe the proper forehand backswing, I wouldn't just tell the student to "take your racquet back as the ball comes over the net." I would have to explain *when* he or she should get the racquet back, how far, what shape he or she should use on the backswing, and why these points are important to the stroke.

If you were to watch me give this type of lesson, you would hear me say one of a number of word-pictures: "Remember the C-shaped backswing!" "Trace a giant egg!" "Try the cane-shaped backswing!" "Take the horseshoe shaped backswing!" The student will catch on to at least one of these concepts. The pro tries one, then another, until he hits on a word-picture that gets results. It's a fun and easy way to learn.

The reader will notice that the word-pictures are arranged with a definite stroke progression in mind. For example, in the forehand chapter, the first illustrations will be on the grips and ready position. The following several pages will address the first-quarter backswing, the completion of the backswing, then the foreswing, and so on. This makes it easy for you to perceive your own mistakes by trial and error; you can try each picture one by one, and by so doing isolate your mistakes and work on them. Use the "buddy system." You might try taking a friend to the tennis court and helping each other find your mistakes.

In this book you have the condensed witticisms, maxims, dictums, and epigrams of the finest teaching tennis professionals in the world. I have collected these word pictures from books, conversation, study, observation, and more than 40,000 hours of lessons on the teaching court.

The game of tennis has not changed that much, but many of the top teaching professionals have passed on, grown old, or are no longer active. Nevertheless, their teaching and word-pictures live on. I would like to give credit here to some of the finest teaching professionals, in my estimation, in the world—past and present. I am crediting their contributions to the academic side of tennis, not just to the playing, managing, promoting, or coaching. They are:

Bill Tilden, Alice Marble "Teach" Tennent, Mercer Beaseley, Rene LaCoste, Jack Kramer, Bill Talbert, Lester Stoefen, Sr., Dick Skeen, Harvey Snodgrass, Walter Westbrook, Helen Wills, J. Parmly Paret, the Dougherty Brothers, Don Budge, Pancho Segura, Pancho Gonzales, Paul Xanthos, Chet and Bill Murphy, John Gardiner, Bob Harmon, Dick Gould, Vic Braden, Jack Barnaby, Eve Kraft, Tim Gallwey, Tom Stow, Dennis Van Der Meer, Billie Jean King, Bobby Riggs, John Newcombe, Alan Metzler, Harry Hopman, Tony Trabert, Perry T. Jones, Ken Rosewall, Rod Laver,

Stan Smith, Joe Bixler, Myron McNamara, Jim Verdieck, Clarence Mabry, Roy Emerson, George Toley, Chris Evert, Fred Stolle, Fred Perry, Gussie Moran, Nancy Chaffee, Little Mo Connally, Arthur Ashe.

There are many more word-pictures than can go into this single paperback. This book contains some of the best mental images dealing with the specific strokes—forehand, backhand, serve-overhead, volley—and with the general areas of net play, strategies, tactics, conditioning, equipment, and mental preparation. This is Volume 1. Other volumes will follow as my syndicated newspaper column continues.

FOREHAND

Teaching pros have several expressions descriptive of the forehand stroke: "It is the first stroke to go and the last one to come back." "The forehand is the workhorse of tennis." "The forehand is the pivot around which one's game is built." "The game can be played with a semi-weak backhand but never with a weak forehand."

The forehand must be understood well and developed through long hours of practice. Many times when world class tournament players go to a teaching pro for help, their problem is on the forehand or forehand return-of-serve. Why? For three major reasons comparable to the backhand side. Let's take a look at these:

1. The racquet goes back with one hand instead of two as on the backhand. (Less feel, sensitivity, and tougher to keep grooved.)
2. When swinging forward on the forehand, the right shoulder is in back of the body. It must swing across

11

the chest area or breadth of the chest. (Even though upper body should turn, nevertheless, some resistance can be encountered.)

3. When hitting a backhand you sight the ball in by simply thinking of an arrow pointed at the ball off your right shoulder (just before contact). On the forehand, the upper body has opened just before contact, not allowing any shoulder point. A lack of feeling for the shot results.

Generally speaking, I think the most common error on the forehand is overrunning the ball, which leads to other problems. Pay attention to the word-pictures on how to keep the ball away from your body.

Pay attention to the explanation of how to use spin on the forehand. Note how little use the chop plays on the forehand, but how important it is to know how to hit over the ball or apply topspin drive to this swing.

Vigilant attention must be given to the "shape" of the backswing on the forehand. There are two correct ways to take the racquet back: the circular backswing and the flat backswing. The one incorrect backswing is also shown. Know this improper swing and its results. I advocate the circular backswing, because I feel it aids rhythm and topspin drive.

Target tennis is important. Note the mental images that help you avoid the chances for error. Do not try to skim the net unless your opponents are attacking. And learn to play the percentages.

Finally, in succession, learn your stroke production, then consistency and accuracy, then depth, and, lastly, know your strategy and tactics. Know the exact role power plays on your forehand, and when to use it.

IN THE FOREHAND READY POSITION, KEEP THE RACQUET IN THE CENTER OF YOUR BODY

1. Avoid losing time on your backswing. Do not favor one side or the other with your racquet or racquet head while in the ready waiting position.

2. Note that the eyes are just above the tip of the racquet head. Avoid cocking your racquet head up so high that it interrupts or blocks your vision.

3. To assume the correct stance, spread your legs and feet about as far as your shoulder span.

GET A HAND ON YOUR EASTERN FOREHAND GRIP

1. Have a friend hand you a racquet, holding it in the position demonstrated here.

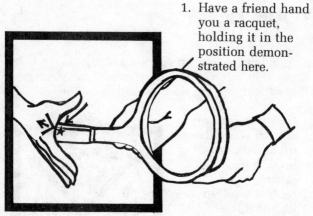

2. When placing your hand on the grip, the "V" formed between the knuckles of your first finger and thumb should be placed on the illustrated star. The arrow going away from the "V" should be pointed to your right shoulder.

3. The Eastern forehand grip is one of the most universally used grips. It's advantageous on low, high and outside balls and good for all surfaces.

THE CONTINENTAL FOREHAND GRIP! GOOD OR BAD?

1. As illustrated in the box, the Continental forehand is characterized by the first knuckle (black dot) being on top of the grip.

2. The grip is used primarily in Europe as well as in Australia, New Zealand, South America and any country with slow court surfaces such as grass, clay, or rubico. On these surfaces, power is not a large factor in winning.

3. Note that with the Continental grip, the player will characteristically hit the ball behind him or opposite the back hip (disadvantage), with lack of power and eye control. With this grip, a player can hit low balls and wide balls well (advantage). However, the difficulty is in the high balls and hitting the ball opposite the front hip for power.

15

DEVELOP THE "C" OR HALF MOON, ALPHABET SWING FOR THE CORRECT CIRCULAR MOTION ON THE FOREHAND

1. This is another way to develop more rhythm, power, smoothness, style, and topspin to your forehand.

2. Watch the Pros, world class players, club champions and local tournament winners. Ninety percent of them will use the orthodox circular swing, leading to smooth graceful impartation of topspin, a crucial element to winning tennis.

EARMARK YOUR CIRCULAR SWING ON THE FOREHAND

1. To begin a correct circular swing, make sure you take the racquet head by your ear on the backswing.

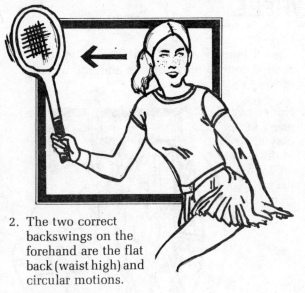

2. The two correct backswings on the forehand are the flat back (waist high) and circular motions.

3. Keep the racquet head up, or above the wrist on the backswing.

TO DEVELOP A GOOD FOREHAND CIRCULAR SWING, THINK OF TRACING THE TOP OF AN IMAGINARY WHEEL

1. A good, properly sized, circular swing will develop rhythm, smoothness, topspin and, ultimately, power to your forehand.

2. Notice how many of the playing professionals on TV use the circular technique.

THE CANE SHAPED FOREHAND BACKSWING

1. One of the two correct backswings on the forehand is the "Flat Back" backswing. The cane mental picture will help develop that technique.

2. Tracing the curl at the end of the cane will help develop rhythm, power, and topspin to your forehand.

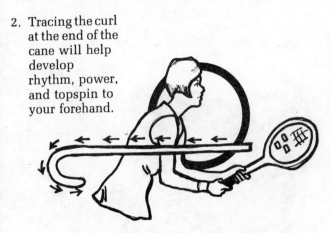

3. The mental picture of the cane should be about waist to chest high.

4. Think of tracing a giant cane as you take your racquet back. Trace it with either your hand or racquet head.

IMAGINE TRACING A GIANT HORSESHOE TO DEVELOP A SMOOTH, CIRCULAR FOREHAND SWING

1. Give yourself more rhythm, style, and topspin by developing a smooth, circular swing with this mental image.

2. The other correct backswing is the flat backswing. However, watch the pros! Note the majority of finished players use the semicircular technique. Beginners and intermediates generally use the flat back technique.

AVOID LEADING WITH TOO MUCH ELBOW ON YOUR FOREHAND BACKSWING OR YOU WILL SUPPRESS YOUR RACQUET FACE

1. The player here has led back with his elbow incorrectly. Note how the racquet face immediately turns downward. The racquet face will have a strong tendency to stay in this "pancake" position throughout the stroke. The player has lost his "edge control" and will most likely hit the ball downward.

2. To correct this negative tendency, try to balance an imaginary coin on the top edge of your racquet in the "ready position"; try to keep the coin balanced throughout the swing.

21

SPIN LIKE A TOP WHEN PREPARING FOREHAND BACKSWING

1. Note how this player is directly side on to the net when the ball comes over. Left hip and shoulder are turned toward the ball.

2. This is similar to the wind up of a baseball pitcher. It will help you "torque" your upper body prior to unwinding into the foreswing.

3. This will help you generate smooth power on your forehand.

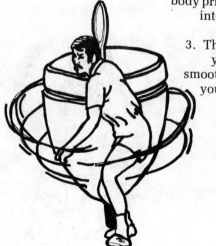

HIDE YOUR RACQUET HAND FROM YOUR OPPONENT FOR THE CORRECT LENGTH ON YOUR BACKSWING

1. Give yourself a definite mental place to go when you take your racquet back. Do not just be satisfied with saying, "get that racquet back." Ask yourself exactly how far should you take the racquet back. By using this technique, you will take it back neither too little nor too much.

23

POINT THE RACQUET BUTT AT THE RIGHT NET POST FOR THE CORRECT LENGTH ON YOUR BACKSWING

1. If you swing back too little on your backswing, your racquet butt will point to your opponent, resulting in a "push" and lack of power.

2. If you exaggerate your backswing too much, you will "spray" your shot, resulting in an out of control shot.

POINT YOUR LEFT SHOULDER AT THE ONCOMING BALL TO INSURE GOOD UPPER BODY TURN

1. This technique will guarantee that the upper body is side on to the net, thus adding power and insuring the correct length on the backswing.

2. The player is stepping diagonally toward the netpost, but still toward the net with the left foot. This step of the left foot insures the lower body turn essential to good percentage tennis.

PROPER BACKSWING DISTANCE

1. Picture a fence behind you. Backswing until racquet hits imaginary fence.

2. Note player's grip hand is hidden; hiding grip hand from opponent will also give proper backswing distance.

3. Bigger backswing means too hard a hit; less means "pushing" the ball.

GET THE BALL IN THE "STRIKE ZONE" ON YOUR FOREHAND

1. The good leverage and most successful forehand is oriented around and about the waist to chest high area like the baseball "strike zone."

2. Hitting the ball in the "strike area" will improve your steadiness, power and control.

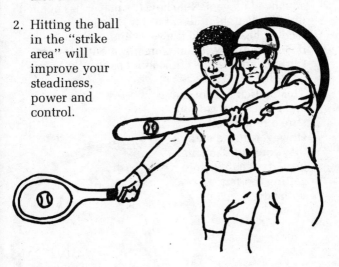

LEARN TO "SLIDE" YOUR FOREHAND DOWN THE LINE! LEAD WITH THE WRIST! HIT LATE!

1. This is a very deceptive shot and advocated for advanced players. Note how the player has opened up with her shoulders, but is "dragging" her racquet head behind the wrist and will hit the ball down the line with an element of outside spin. Chris Evert executes this shot beautifully.

2. This particular shot can add great variety to your stroke repertoire. However, make sure that your fundamental game is secure before getting too fancy with advanced shots.

DEVELOP A SWEEPING FINISH ON YOUR FOREHAND

1. To correct your forehand follow-through, imagine sweeping six bottles off a table that is slanted very gradually up.

2. This technique will correct a strong tendency to pull across your body or ball at contact.

3. This mental picture will help the racquet face follow the trajectory of the ball after contact, improving accuracy and depth.

AVOID CHICKEN WINGING OR SHOVELING YOUR FOREHAND

1. When you take the ball too close to your body it will cause you to bend your elbow, referred to in instructional jargon as "Chicken Wing" caused by an "inside pitch."

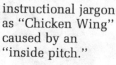

2. A "Chicken Wing" will cause you to drop your racquet head, resulting in a "Shoveling" of your shot, which will elevate the ball too much.

3. When you "cramp" your shot you will also take the ball behind your body or too late. Note how the ball has passed behind the player's visual point. All caused by a bent elbow.

30

PRACTICE HITTING YOUR FOREHAND WITH A MENTAL HOLE IN THE CENTER OF THE STRINGS

1. Improve your ability to "hit through" the ball for better accuracy and for more "solid" contact.

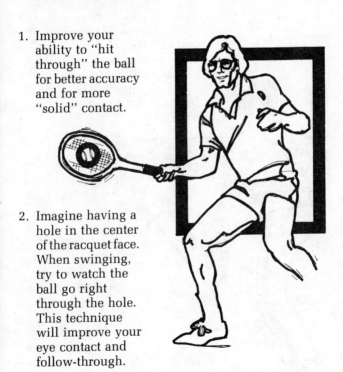

2. Imagine having a hole in the center of the racquet face. When swinging, try to watch the ball go right through the hole. This technique will improve your eye contact and follow-through.

FOR IDEAL FOOTWORK ON THE FOREHAND, STEP TOWARD THE RIGHT NETPOST

1. When you use this word picture, you will find that you have weight going both toward the net, and still towards the ball. This technique will lead to more solid impact with better balance.

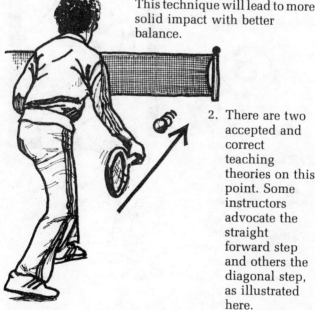

2. There are two accepted and correct teaching theories on this point. Some instructors advocate the straight forward step and others the diagonal step, as illustrated here.

PRACTICE WATCHING THE SPOT WHERE CONTACT WAS MADE TO AVOID PULLING YOUR EYES OFF THE BALL

1. As you practice following through on your forehand, also practice keeping your head and eyes set on the spot where you made contact. Golfers also use this technique when teeing off to keep from pulling their heads up.

2. This good eye concentration will improve your ability to take the ball right on the "sweet spot" of the center of the strings.

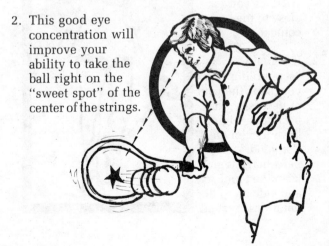

KEEP THE BACK FOOT ANCHORED WHILE HITTING THROUGH YOUR FOREHAND

1. Avoid bringing the back foot around while the racquet makes contact. If you step into the ball with your back foot it will put you too close to the ball at contact.

2. If you are "scrambling" for your shot, then out of necessity, the back foot might have to step out. For good percentage tennis, keep the foot back and side on to the net unless rushed.

AVOID "SITTING" WHEN PLAYING YOUR FOREHAND; DO NOT LET THE BALL "PUSH" YOU

1. Note the player is on his heels. He has allowed the ball to "press" him by hitting late, or allowing the ball to come too far before execution of the stroke.

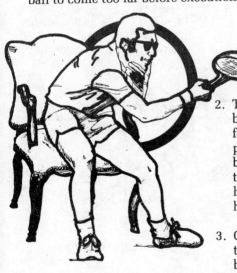

2. This backward balance will force the player to error by "popping" the ball up or hitting too high.

3. Counteract this tendency by hitting the ball out in front of the body or front foot.

DO NOT "FALL" TO YOUR FOREHAND, "STEP" TO IT

The Advantages of the Step Are:

1. Better Balance.

2. Guarantees the side is on to the net. (Closed stance)

3. Transfers the weight into the shot.

4. Player can push back faster to the ready position.

5. Player can reach further more comfortably.

INCORRECT➤   ◄CORRECT

HIT THE BALL AT 9 O'CLOCK FOR A MORE SOLID FOREHAND

1. This mental picture will help to cock the top edge of the racquet head up level with the wrist.

2. If you drop the racquet head to 8 o'clock or lower, your wrist will become progressively looser, resulting in loss of solid impact and pace on the ball.

3. Dropping wrist will result in shot going too high.

"ROCK" ONTO THAT LEFT FOOT AS YOU EXECUTE YOUR FOREHAND DRIVE

1. Whenever possible, try to get yourself arranged, set up, positioned so that you can rock solidly onto your left foot while making contact.

2. This transference of weight will give you added power with less effort. It will also give your ball "heavy momentum."

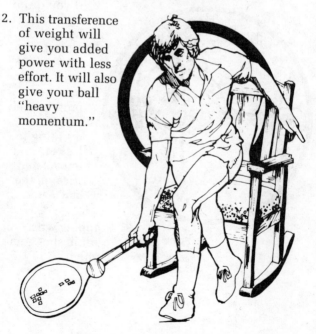

CONTROL YOUR RACQUET FACE ON THE HIGH OFFENSIVE FOREHAND. USE THE MENTAL IMAGE OF A PLATE FOR BETTER TECHNIQUE

1. Note that on the high forehand, the player "tilts" his racquet face a bit downward like the top of the imaginary plate. He is offending the shot and hitting it hard with topspin.

2. If the ball were lower, chest to knee high, his racquet face would be flush to the ball, like the center of the plate.

3. If the ball were lower than knee high, his racquet face would "tilt" slightly up, like the bottom of the plate. This technique will improve your steadiness.

DEVELOP A GOOD FOREHAND DOWN-THE-LINE SHOT. PRACTICE HITTING, THEN POINTING THE RACQUET HEAD AT THE TARGET

1. Ninety per cent of your opponents will be right-handed. The ability to hit the ball down the line is essential. In beginning, intermediate and club tennis, this is generally the weakest side for players. Exploit it! Play the "coffin corner"—the backhand corner.

2. It is 17 feet shorter down the line than crosscourt. This shot demands practice and is the mark of the skilled player.

DEVELOP A TOPSPIN FOREHAND! IMAGINE "BRUSHING" OR "SWEEPING" YOUR RACQUET HEAD UP THE BACK OF THE BALL

1. Pretend you have a sandpaper Ping-Pong paddle and a ball. Brush up the back of the ball briskly and it will cause the ball to "dip."

2. All players of any significance have the ability to hit "over" the ball (topspin). Topspin will enable you to hit the ball higher over the net and still hold it in the court.

3. Topspin is applied by making your racquet face travel from low to high in relation to the oncoming level of the ball.

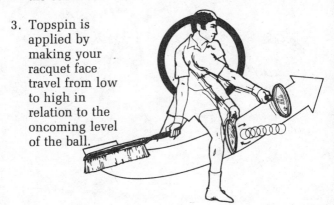

MAY RACQUET HEAD DROP BELOW THE WRIST?

1. Almost never. Keep the top edge of the racquet level with the wrist. To get lower, bend the knees more.

2. Top A players and pros are exceptions. Gardnar Mulloy, Jack Kramer, Bjorn Borg and Guillermo Vilas break this rule regularly with spectacular results. Others should stick to the proper technique.

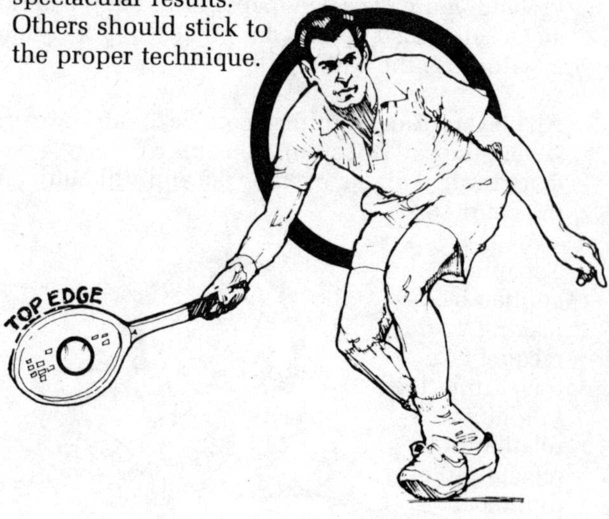

TOP EDGE

42

HIT THE BALL AT THE PEAK OF THE BOUNCE FOR A MORE EFFECTIVE FOREHAND. MOVE TO THE BALL!

1. It is a mark of "court savvy" and experience when a player moves into the court to take the ball either on the rise or at the peak of the bounce.

2. Too many players will "lay back" incorrectly, and allow the ball to fall off the peak of the bounce, almost to their feet.

3. Allowing the ball to fall gives your opponent more time to get set and causes errors by your hitting the ball "off your shoelaces."

AVOID OVERDONE FOLLOW-THROUGH ON FOREHAND

1. It's correct to "open up" or turn when completing the forehand. But a radical revolving as illustrated will cause an error.

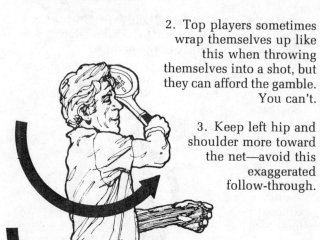

2. Top players sometimes wrap themselves up like this when throwing themselves into a shot, but they can afford the gamble. You can't.

3. Keep left hip and shoulder more toward the net—avoid this exaggerated follow-through.

LEARN TO ACCENTUATE YOUR FOREHAND TOPSPIN. "ROLL" YOUR WRIST AND RACQUET HEAD ON THE FOLLOW-THROUGH AS IF YOU WERE "BATTING A BASEBALL "

1. Teaching pros advocate this technique for finished or advanced students. However, beginners or intermediates should make sure they are under the close supervision of a pro when they begin to attempt this shot or it can lead to some bad habits.

2. Remember! Topspin can be applied by a "low to high" stroke with a "flush" racquet face. This technique is designed to give the ball added length and radical topspin. This shot has a strong chance for error when used before being aware of the pitfalls.

AVOID THE BANANA SWING ON YOUR FOREHAND

1. The one incorrect swing on the forehand is when you drop your racquet head below your waist level on the backswing or foreswing.

2. A "Banana Swing" will elevate your shot, involuntarily causing you to hit high.

3. If by mistake you trace the Banana with your racquet head you will be "Scooping", "Spooning", "Dipping" or "Golfing" your shot incorrectly.

BACKHAND

In the beginning stages, most players find the backhand, as opposed to the forehand, the more difficult stroke. However, as the player progresses, the backhand becomes the easiest.

There are four stumbling blocks on the backhand that show up sooner or later in almost everyone's game. They are:

1. A tendency to overrun the ball.
2. An inclination to not turn enough toward the side fence as the ball comes to the backhand.
3. A propensity to swing the racquet and front shoulder radically to the right when executing the backhand (right-handed backhand).
4. A strong tendency to "chop" the ball rather than drive the shot.

On the backhand side, players tend to chop the ball from the beginning stages on through the development of their game. The chop is correct if you know when, where, and how to use it. It can be used to control, confuse, or defend. But it should never be used on every shot. Learn to drive the ball as well as chop.

Since players usually pick up the racquet with their right hands in the beginning stages, they tend to hit more balls on the forehand than on the backhand side. Since the forehand gets more use and feels more comfortable, it's logical that most people, when practicing or playing, drop the ball on their forehand and hit it over the net to their partner—this constitutes thousands of balls hit off the forehand. The poor backhand gets left behind! Players will compound the problem by running around the backhand and hitting a forehand instead, because their forehand feels more comfortable. Avoid this habit! In practice, run around your forehand to hit your backhand. Always feed the ball off your backhand side. This little hint helps keep the backhand practiced.

The two-handed backhand is very popular now. Students often ask me if they should switch to a two-handed backhand. My pat answer to this is, "If it's natural for you, go to it, but never take a natural one-handed shot and change it to an unnatural two-hander." Unfortunately, too many people see a champion use it and go for the look of the stroke rather than what is best suited to them.

The backhand return-of-serve is basically the same as the groundstroke, with two deviations. The backswing shape and distance should be shortened for the return-of-serve, and an effort should be made to hit the ball earlier than on the groundstroke. The backhand return-of-serve (particularly off the forehand side of the court) is one of the most difficult shots in the game, yet it's the least practiced. Avoid starting a rally from baseline to baseline. Have your practice partner hit serves to your backhand return to start the rally. Always practice your weakest area.

CORRECT SERVE AND BACKHAND GRIP

1. Another mental image to help you assume the proper grip!

2. Remember! Grips have the greatest influence over the racquet face at contact. The ball will go where the racquet face is looking.

3. Try bouncing a ball toward the ground with the bottom edge of your racquet (it will feel unnatural to use a forehand grip).

4. Your hand will automatically move toward a Continental (hatchet grip) which is the correct service or backhand grip.

CONTINENTAL-BACKHAND GRIP ON SERVE

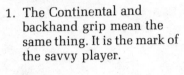

1. The Continental and backhand grip mean the same thing. It is the mark of the savvy player.

2. Beginners can—and do—cheat to a forehand grip on serve (dot moves to the right). But progressing players should use the correct service grip (dot aligned with dark area indicated on grip).

3. To serve well, you must eventually adapt and be comfortable with the Continental.

4. Knowing and using the correct serve grip teaches you the correct backhand grip.

FOUR-STEP BACKHAND GRIP

1. Assume the regular handshake grip for your eastern forehand.

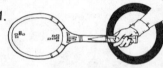

2. Now form a lump in the wrist of your racquet hand.

3. Turn your right hand to the left until the lump disappears (do not turn the racquet).

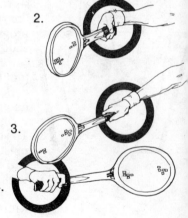

4. You now have a correct backhand grip. Extend first finger as if it were a trigger finger to a pistol, and get ready to shoot that punishing shot!

IN THE "READY POSITION" MAINTAIN YOUR POSITION "THREE FEET" BEHIND THE BASELINE

1. This player is obviously playing doubles since he is close to the forehand or right side of the court. For singles he would be behind the center mark.

2. Often, players will incorrectly stand on the baseline or inside of it. Observers find his mistake characteristic of beginners or intermediates. "Bad" court position like this will result in many errors as a consequence of balls bouncing at your feet.

3. The bigger percentage of balls hit to you will bounce between the service line and baseline. If you are in bad court position you will play balls at your feet with a high degree of difficulty.

53

WHY IS THIS PLAYER BOUNCING ON HIS TOES AND FAVORING HIS BACKHAND IN THE READY POSITION?

1. He is returning serve! Many teaching pros advocate bouncing lightly on the toes or balls of the feet to avoid a flat footed ready position which results in a slow start with the footwork.

2. When returning serve it is an accepted technique to favor the backhand side with the racquet head. It is also acceptable to wait with the backhand grip. Beginning, intermediate and many "club players" have a more difficult time getting their grip changed and racquet back on the backhand return of serve. This is a comfortable and time-saving technique.

WHY IS THIS PLAYER BENT SO LOW IN THE READY POSITION? IS IT CORRECT?

1. The exaggerated low bend indicates the player is returning serve, and most likely it is a first serve. This technique is correct and you will observe top players using it. In this class of play the first serve usually comes in low, sliding, heavy and fast.

2. You will note on second serves the player will take two or more steps forward and stand up a bit more. The second serve will generally be slower, have spin and tend to bounce higher.

EARMARK BACKHAND

1. Pass racquet head opposite left ear when setting up backhand.

2. This starts a smooth, rhythmic, circular swing and helps put racquet head below oncoming ball to hit up the back for topspin drive.

3. From this position, player can stop racquet head high and chop down for backswing.

4. This helps keep racquet head higher than wrist.

SEAT TO NET

1. Exaggerate turn before hitting backhand. Lefthanders are particularly guilty of not turning.

2. Guarantee your turn by moving seat at least ¼ to the net and moving shoulders so you are looking over front shoulder.

3. Step toward left net post as you execute.

4. Point right shoulder at ball.

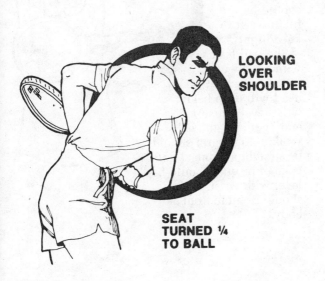

LOOKING OVER SHOULDER

SEAT TURNED ¼ TO BALL

CHICKEN WINGS

1. Preparing her backhand, the player has bent both arms at the elbows. Teachers call this "chicken wings."

2. This results in two common errors:
—The girl will hit at chest to shoulder high level (the ball should be hit at waist to knee high).
—She will lead with an elbow at contact. Racquet head will drop below wrist level "pushing" and "golfing" the ball weakly. Right arm should be straight at contact, top edge of racquet should be level with wrist. Ball should be hit in front of body.

WRIST ANGLE

1. Upper illustration shows most common error on the backhand groundstroke. The sharp angle between wrist and racquet head is too radical. (If chopping or slicing, this technique is correct.) Racquet head is cocked too high.

2. It's allowable to take the racquet head back high, but remember to drop the head (lower illustration) down to the oncoming level of ball (should be chest to knee high) then hit forward with a gradual "sweeping" motion upward.

**INCORRECT
UNLESS
CHOPPING
OR
SLICING**

CORRECT

SHOULDER-HIP GUIDE DIRECTION

1. Where hips and shoulders are pointed generally dictates where the ball will go on a backhand.

2. This player's partially open stance (right foot has not crossed over back foot) indicates his shot will go to the backhand corner (where arrows are pointed).

3. When hitting down the line turn hip and shoulder (exaggerate).

   Make sure you step across back foot (step to left net post with right foot). Hit away from body with closed stance.

DRAW A SWORD

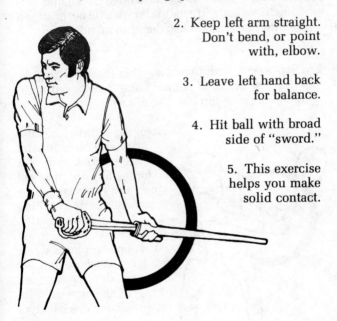

1. On forward swing of backhand, pull on racquet grip as if drawing a sword.

2. Keep left arm straight. Don't bend, or point with, elbow.

3. Leave left hand back for balance.

4. Hit ball with broad side of "sword."

5. This exercise helps you make solid contact.

TWO-HANDED BACKHAND— YES OR NO?

1. Yes. It is as good as a one-handed backhand; sometimes better if a natural stroke. Do not change a natural one-handed backhand to an educated two-hander.

2. Grip is with both hands together (baseball grip) or with first finger of bottom hand interlocked with baby finger of top hand (golf grip).

3. Note player has a forehand grip with bottom hand (knuckle position indicates forehand grip). It is not necessary to change to a backhand grip if hitting a two hander.

4. If one-hander is weak, insecure and not developing, then experiment with two-hander. See if it gives you confidence (preferably under the eye of a pro). It can add more power.

STAND UP BACKHAND

1. Incorrect! The easiest error to make on the backhand groundstroke: This player has addressed the ball too close, and too late!

2. Note there is no knee bend. Thus the player must drop her racquet head, resulting in a "golfed" shot which invariably goes long.

3. Although the player may be lobbing (forced to hit easy because of low racquet head), the top edge of racquet head should be cocked up almost level with wrist. The knees must be bent to get the racquet head up.

4. Even lobbing, the player is likely to hit (golf) ball over baseline.

NO SITTING

1. The player is falling away from her shot as if she were tired and wanted to sit down.

2. This will cause errors wide of court or into the net.

3. To correct this tendency think of leaning into the right knee (balanced) as if you were getting up out of the couch.

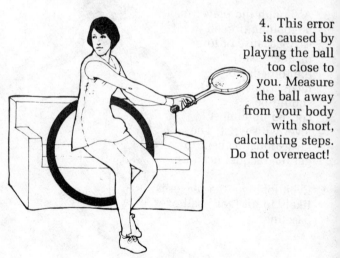

4. This error is caused by playing the ball too close to you. Measure the ball away from your body with short, calculating steps. Do not overreact!

IRON OUT BACKHAND

1. Many tend to pull up on the backhand stroke too soon. When players feel the ball on the strings they will mysteriously jerk the racquet head up and pull it across to the right.

2. Nip this bad habit! Imagine hitting along the top of an ironing board. Keep the ball on the strings as you sweep along the level top of the board, then lift gradually with the racquet head to about shoulder or head height or slightly higher than head height.

STIFF KNEE

1. This player's front knee is stiff. Rigid leg keeps his eyes too far from ball level to visually groove into ball and feel shot.

2. Lack of knee bend further prevents weight from flowing into shot at impact. He tends to sit back rather than shifting into shot.

3. Stiff knee is common bad habit in backhand volleys and groundstrokes. Often caused by overreacting and getting too close—ball then stands you up.

3 O'CLOCK BACKHAND

1. This image helps keep wrist firm at contact. Drop racquet head to 4 or 5 and note how loose wrist is.

2. Think of the clockface as being a foot in front of you.

3. Hit ball opposite front hip, or earlier. This means good eye contact and weight behind the shot.

4. Dropping head to 4 or 5 will result in shots hit too high, often causing errors long.

BACK TO WALL BACKHAND

1. Common mistake is bending at waist instead of knees.

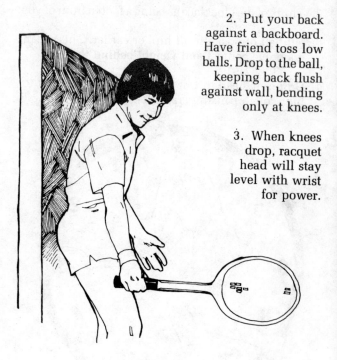

2. Put your back against a backboard. Have friend toss low balls. Drop to the ball, keeping back flush against wall, bending only at knees.

3. When knees drop, racquet head will stay level with wrist for power.

RUN AROUND BACKHAND TO HIT FOREHAND?

1. Question as old as the game. Some players possess a better backhand than forehand.

2. Generally, if you feel comfortable and the shot can reasonably be pulled off, it's okay to run around and hit your strong forehand.

3. Warning! Make sure you can reply offensively, otherwise you will be caught in the backhand corner and passed on the forehand side.

HANGING ARMS

1. The adult player's two-handed backhand is correct because she has position on the ball to play it waist high, 3 to 4 feet away. Both elbows and arms are hanging comfortably straight. She will get better accuracy, power.

2. The junior player is incorrectly playing the ball too high and too close, causing bent elbows! Her shot will be weak and shallow.

FENCE WITH OPPONENT—PROBE WEAKNESSES

1. Even during warmup, find opponent's weaknesses. Check out backhand.

2. Most club and recreational players will be weakest on the backhand.

3. If you find weak forehand or backhand, attack it ruthlessly. "Fence" until you get your chance, then move in for the kill.

4. Remember the strategy of "hitting to their strength (forehand) to get to their weakness (backhand)."

FRISBEE BACKHAND

1. Picture throwing a Frisbee.

2. Note how the Frisbee thrower is flipping the back of his hand away from his body. If he had a tennis racquet in hand this technique would be called "hitting out" at the ball.

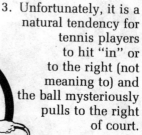

3. Unfortunately, it is a natural tendency for tennis players to hit "in" or to the right (not meaning to) and the ball mysteriously pulls to the right of court.

4. Correct this tendency by turning your seat and shoulders toward the ball and exaggerate "hitting out."

TOSS THE HAT

1. Are your backhands going out of court, or wide to opponent's backhand side (when in fact you are trying to hit down-the-line to their forehand)?

2. This common error happens more on the backhand side than the forehand (the tendency to swing your racquet across your body to the right is stronger on the backhand).

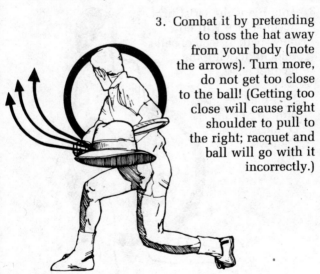

3. Combat it by pretending to toss the hat away from your body (note the arrows). Turn more, do not get too close to the ball! (Getting too close will cause right shoulder to pull to the right; racquet and ball will go with it incorrectly.)

WRIST BELOW RACQUET HEAD

1. Keep wrist below racquet head on groundstroke backhand as well as volley.

2. Beginning and intermediate players find this makes for a solid hit.

3. This keeps the wrist firm. Racquet face will now move ball, instead of ball's velocity moving the racquet head.

4. This player properly bends at knees, rather than waist.

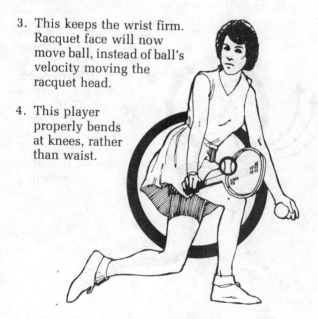

THE HIGH BACKHAND

1. Hopefully, you would have better position than this. Back up to take the ball waist to chest high, or move up to take it on the rise before it gets out of the "strike zone."

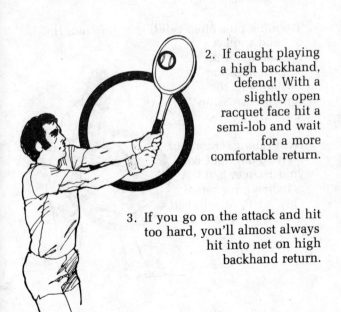

2. If caught playing a high backhand, defend! With a slightly open racquet face hit a semi-lob and wait for a more comfortable return.

3. If you go on the attack and hit too hard, you'll almost always hit into net on high backhand return.

DEAL THE CARD

1. Get the feeling of hitting away from your body on the backhand.

2. Pretend you are dealing a giant card away from your stomach.

3. Teaching pros often call this hitting out. Hit out and contact the ball opposite your front hip or earlier. Note the right foot crossing correctly.

4. Avoid going across your body to the right with your racquet hand. A common error called "hitting in," it pulls ball involuntarily to the right.

BEND AT KNEES

1. On low ball player's back knee almost touches ground as knees bend correctly!

2. If you bend at waist and lock your knees, head and eyes will "tilt" causing bad court perspective.

3. Note how player's eyes stay horizontal to the net; racquet head stays up correctly due to good knee bend. (If the player bends at waist, racquet head will drop, "golfing" the ball.)

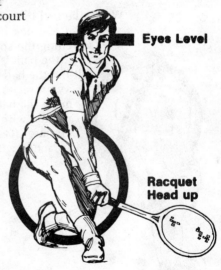

Eyes Level

Racquet Head up

DEADLY EYE CONCENTRATION

1. This player is doing what most do not: watching the ball. Head and eyes are right on the ball to contact. You've heard teaching pros yell, "Read the label on the ball."

2. "Watch the ball to the racquet face and watch it leave it," "Keep watching the spot where you hit the ball." These tips aid in hitting the ball more solidly. "If your racquet had no strings make the ball go through the middle without touching the frame." (Good ball machine practice with an old frame).

THROW AWAY RACQUET

1. Practice good backhand follow-through for depth, accuracy, power.

2. Pretend you are hitting a backhand, then throw racquet after the ball as it leaves the strings. Note how arm straightens out.

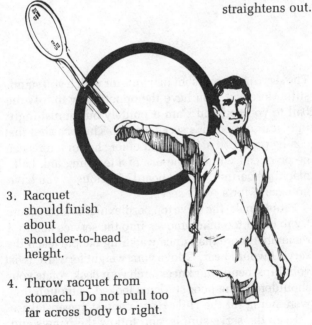

3. Racquet should finish about shoulder-to-head height.

4. Throw racquet from stomach. Do not pull too far across body to right.

THE SERVE AND OVERHEAD

The serve is the one shot in tennis for which you stand still. Moreover, you have the opportunity to toss the ball to yourself and slam it politely but punishingly into your opponent's service court. This is a shot that can be practiced alone. What other shot in tennis can be practiced without the use of a teaching aid, ball machine, partner, or backboard? Obviously, you have no excuse for a weak serve.

People make the serve too perplexing. Even teachers try to build too many moves into the service action. I remember more than once watching people teach the serve. I would hear, "Move your weight forward, twist your hips, bend your knees, arch your back, rotate your shoulders." The poor students looked as though they were going for the Hula Hoop contest sweepstakes.

Keep the serve simple, and follow the panels and word-pictures in this section. I can almost guarantee success. A lot of moves on the serve are natural. A good example: Try arching your back and your knees will automatically bend. Why should I confuse the student by making him think about this, when it happens naturally?

Dump the beginner grip as soon as possible. There isn't a class player in the world who serves with a forehand grip. A forehand, or beginning, grip will be forever limiting throughout your development—you will never serve good spin with a forehand grip, and you cannot be a sophisticated player without spin.

Know your spins well, and be able to produce them at will. Again, spin is used to control, defend, and confuse. What good is a baseball pitcher if he cannot keep the batter off-balance with curves, knuckle balls, and sliders, in addition to fast balls?

If you are going to make errors on your serve, it is better to serve too deep than too shallow. Be courageous! Always practice with depth. The same goes for the overhead smash. The greatest percentage of errors on the serve and overhead consists of hitting into the net. This is caused by mentally "tightening up." Learn to relax in your practice and playing.

The overhead smash is much like a serve, except you don't have the advantage of tossing the ball yourself. Also, the backswing is shorter. The overhead is the final kill—a good player knows that if the ball is lobbed, he will usually win the point. Unfortunately, most people never "oil" the overhead until they are in a match that counts. Practice the overhead incessantly against the ball machine or another player. The overhead smash is not a difficult shot. It can be mastered with practice. You cannot do without it!

HOW TO HOLD FOR TOSS

1. Thumb and first two fingers hold ball to be tossed. Second is cradled in palm.

2. Acceptable current technique is to hold only one ball, put other in pocket.

3. Service success lies 70% in the toss. It must be meticulous.

4. Don't throw away second ball while first is in play.

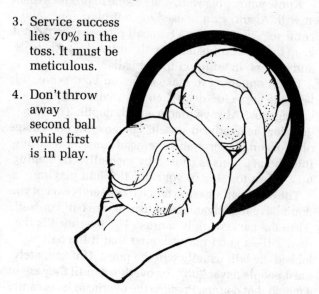

RIGHT HAND AWAY FROM BODY AT READY

1. Ready to serve, this player correctly has both hands to the right of her body.

2. This minimizes chance of error on toss; she will swing back with no interference from her torso.

3. Toss should go above and in front of right shoulder. Left hand is correctly positioned for toss.

ARROW PRINCIPLE

1. In service ready stance, draw imaginary arrow from back fence, through back toe, through front toe. Arrow points to where service will probably go.

2. Thus we see this player is aiming for the backhand corner of the backhand court.

3. Use this arrow principle to aim in practice, so that it lines up automatically in a match.

SIGHT YOUR SERVE LIKE A RIFLE

1. A comfortable ready position isn't enough; be educated.

2. Point or "aim" racquet toward target you are serving to.

3. This helps plot a correct backswing. Form a positive habit: start your serve with the same ready position each time.

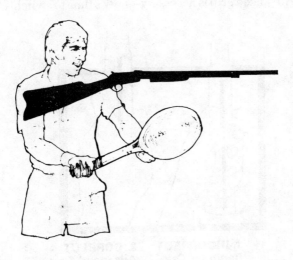

DUMP BEGINNER GRIP!

1. Only the greenest should serve with this grip. Get rid of it.

2. You can't snap wrist with it—butt will fight the hand. You'll continue to pop or float ball for deep errors.

3. Advanced grip is hard to get comfortable with, but worth it. It allows wrist snap, which means spin and power.

4. Advanced grip is necessary—now's time to switch!

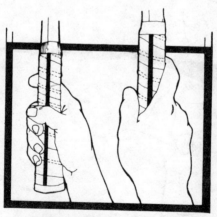

1. INCORRECT
Beginner Grip

2. CORRECT
Advanced Grip

TOSS PRACTICE DRILL

1. Assume correct ready position.

2. Place an old racquet in front of baseline. Face should be in front of left toe.

3. Toss ball so that when it falls back to earth it will strike racquet face on ground.

4. This requires toss slightly right of center body and just in front of baseline.

DROP BOTH HANDS

1. In ready position, begin service toss by dropping racquet hand and toss hand together.

2. Hands separate between waist and knee. Left hand starts toss, racquet hand pulls back.

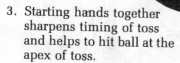

3. Starting hands together sharpens timing of toss and helps to hit ball at the apex of toss.

SLOW AND EASY

1. Draw racquet back and toss ball s-l-o-w-l-y.

2. This makes you more aware of your tossing arm, which leads to accuracy.

3. Jerking the toss looks amateurish.

4. Forget the word "toss." Try "push" or "shove."

ICE CREAM CONE TOSS

1. Accurate toss is 70% of a successful serve.

2. Too low, high, back, forward, left or right spoils serve.

3. Use mental image of ice cream cone with ball balanced on top.

4. Push toss straight up without disturbing ball on imaginary cone.

5. This mental drill helps steady tossing hand, avoid wrist motion.

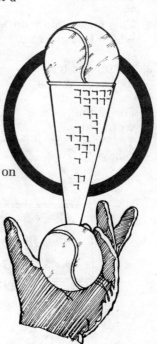

"ELEVATE" SERVICE TOSS

1. Imagine balancing an elevator car full of little people as you toss.

2. Boost ball up through the "elevator shaft" without touching the shaft or jarring the passengers.

3. This mental image helps avoid jerk or flip of ball. Use whole arm: push, shove, boost gently.

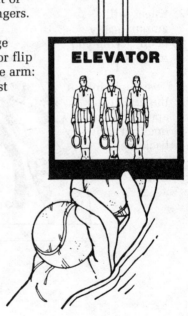

ARCH BACK FOR SERVE POWER

1. "Gang up" under ball in trophy pose. Just before contact, arch back for coiled power.

2. Knees will automatically bend, giving you more spring.

3. Toss high, hit the ball at the apex. Low ball does not allow back arch.

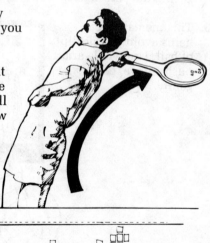

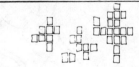

TROPHY POSE PAUSE

1. Some pros like a continuous motion with the racquet head on service; other pros like a slight mental pause as pictured. Both are correct.

2. The slight pause will work better for those who tend to swing at the ball while the toss is on the "rise." The pause will allow the ball to "sit still" at the apex of the toss as you execute with more solidness.

3. Additionally, the pause will help people who have a tendency to toss too high. It will help stop uncomfortable reaching.

93

SPREAD YOUR WINGS

1. Players tend to abbreviate service backswing, or detour directly to the trophy pose.

2. Take full backswing—racquet down past toes, ball hand to waist level.

3. Pretend you have wings. As you toss spread wings fully. You can't exaggerate this technique.

4. Full swing assures smooth, accurate toss and good momentum and rhythm of racquet.

5. Top pros—men and women—do this. Check it out at next big pro match you see in person or on TV.

FOUR STEPS

The service is doing many things with coordination. Simplify it into four steps.

1. Rest weight on back foot before toss.

2. Lightly shift weight to front foot and toss. Don't overshift weight and lose balance. Gang up under the ball.

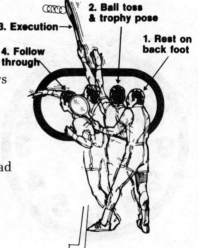

2. Ball toss & trophy pose

3. Execution →

4. Follow through

1. Rest on back foot

3. Now weight flows over baseline. Shoulder, trunk, arm and racquet lean into ball together. Wrist snaps racquet head forward.

4. Finish on left of body.

   When practicing, count off the four steps.

BE A CLOCKWATCHER

1. Use three different tosses for three serves. Use mental image of a clock.

2. Twist: Toss to 12, brush racquet face up and across ball, left to right. Ball kicks to right. Finish on right of body.

3. Flat: Toss to 1. Hit up and directly over ball. Ball goes straight with overspin. Finish on left of body.

4. Slice: Toss to 2. Carve, peel, slice around outside edge of ball. Finish on left of body. Ball curves to left.

BACK COMB TWIST

1. In this serve, racquet face moves from left to right, finishing on right of body causing a reverse spin. Ball kicks to right.

2. Think of combing up the back of the ball and across it with a giant comb.

3. Generally a second serve. A bit passe today: it's tiring to the back and good players will move in on it. But a handy weapon for variety.

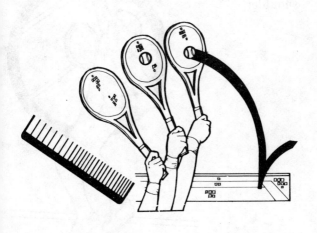

THREE TOSSES

1. Watch the pros. Their topspin, flat or slice serves each command a different toss. But they look the same—object is to fool the opponent.

2. Toss can be 70% of serve's success. Practice incessantly.

3. Whole arm should work as a unit from the shoulder.

TOPSPIN
(KICK)

FLAT

SLICE

CHOOSING SPIN

1. The accomplished player controls the spin on serve. He knows where to toss.

2. Twist: Racquet face travels from 7 to 1 or 2. Wrist snap brushes racquet head up and over. Ball will hop to right.

3. Flat: Wrist snaps at 12. Ball hops straight with overspin.

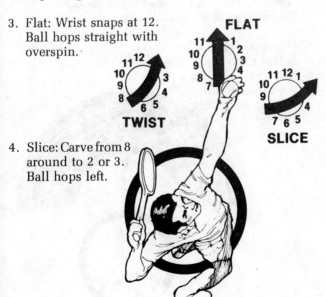

4. Slice: Carve from 8 around to 2 or 3. Ball hops left.

THE RAINBOW SERVE

1. This mental picture helps maintain a smooth pattern on the continuance of your racquet head (after contact) on serve and overhead smash.

2. Players often tighten up at contact and rake the racquet head radically downward and toward their stomach, resulting in errors into the net (jackknifing at waist also causes this).

3. Hit up and over the ball at contact! Make sure you trace the rainbow fully, particularly after contact.

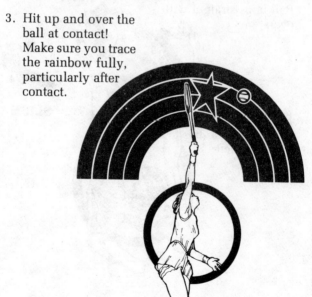

CRACK THE WHIP

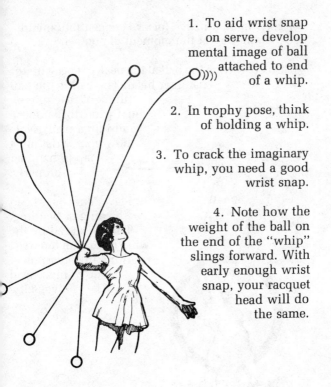

1. To aid wrist snap on serve, develop mental image of ball attached to end of a whip.

2. In trophy pose, think of holding a whip.

3. To crack the imaginary whip, you need a good wrist snap.

4. Note how the weight of the ball on the end of the "whip" slings forward. With early enough wrist snap, your racquet head will do the same.

HAMMER NAIL SERVE

1. A good mental image for eye concentration and service motion at the moment of contact.

2. Think of hitting the ball at the peak of toss with the hammer head. The ball is the nail (think of reaching on your tip toes to hammer a nail into a wall). Note how your wrist must snap to hammer properly.

3. Player's racquet head is bowing or bending. This is caused by the whip or snap of the wrist resulting in better power due to high head velocity.

102

DON'T JACKKNIFE

1. As he makes contact, this player is bent at the waist—jackknifed. A low toss and mental tightening up caused this contortion.

2. His center of gravity (seat) is moving backward while he is trying to hit the ball forward.

3. Back foot will not come over line, meaning lost power and depth.

4. Stand up and extend into the serve! Hit over the ball! Hit up into the ball!

KICK AND SNAP

1. As this player's wrist snaps the serve, his back (right) foot is crossing the line.

2. Body bulk, shoulder, arm, wrist and racquet head are moving together, in one smooth unit. This means maximum power with minimum effort.

3. Practice this, and notice the feeling of fluid coordination.

4. Let racquet head work for you; don't struggle for it.

SLICE PATTERN

1. Seeing is believing. Try to visualize the slice serve. At (1) racquet head hits up and over.

2. Racquet face slightly diagonal at contact. Pros call this carving, peeling or hatchet position.

3. Racquet has hit through impact point with wrist.

4. Follow through. Ball will spin left. Usually a second serve.

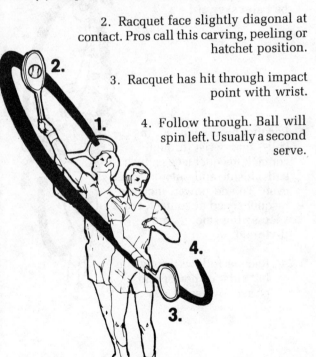

105

CANNONBALL (FLAT) SERVE

1. Racquet face points up at ball—racquet hand should be palm skyward.

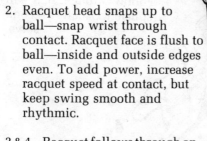

2. Racquet head snaps up to ball—snap wrist through contact. Racquet face is flush to ball—inside and outside edges even. To add power, increase racquet speed at contact, but keep swing smooth and rhythmic.

3 & 4. Racquet follows through on left side for power and correct overspin.

BRING BACK FOOT OVER

1. Back foot should clear line at impact with ball during serve.

2. This brings weight into shot giving better depth. It gives one-stride advantage toward taking the net.

3. Failure to bring foot over means errors into the net and mis-hits on racquet tip, plus poor balance and power.

AVOID STRAINING ELBOW ON SERVE

1. This player is wrong. Racquet head at follow through should end up on opposite side of body.

2. Try this wrong way in practice. You'll feel a definite strain on the elbow.

3. Racquet head should flow across the body and finish on the opposite side from where the serve was hit.

FOLLOW THROUGH ON SERVE

1. Don't pattycake, pancake, baby or pop your service—don't hit, then stop the racquet in mid-flight.

2. Finish with racquet well on your left side.

3. Put your weight into it. Let your body fall or flow into the court.

OVERHEAD SECRETS

1. When preparing a smash, don't take racquet down past toes as in a serve—cock it quickly, as if hefting a hatchet.

2. Draw right foot back as you cock arm. This puts you sideways to the net, as on a serve.

3. Remember: An overhead is just like serve—only you don't get to toss it yourself.

DON'T TRIP!

1. Don't use bad footwork when covering a lob with an overhead.

2. Don't face the net and backpeddle. That is the slowest way to move back and leads to injury (looks like an amateur or beginner). It's easy to trip and sit on your ankles.

3. Try not to run one foot over the other (illustrated) unless horribly hurried. Player could easily trip himself.

4. Learn to lead back with right foot (puts side on to the net) and side slide. Watch the pros on T.V. It's a quicker, smoother, safer way of going back.

THE OTHER HAND

1. A crucial technique on the overhead smash. Watch any pro. They always do this.

2. Why does the left hand point at the ball?

   A. As the player fades back to hit, it gives him balance (try hitting an overhead with the left hand in your pocket).

   B. He judges the ball (sights it in) with his left hand.

   C. If necessary, the player will use the hand to shade the sun.

3. Note how player is side on to net. Try not to back up and execute facing the net.

CUP THAT OVERHEAD

1. At contact on the overhead smash, tremendous wrist snap is demanded.

2. To guarantee wrist snap, form an imaginary cup between racquet tip and your chest. Use this same secret on your serve. Make sure tip leads wrist on follow-through.

3. Wrist snap will give ball added forward spin and power (without spin the velocity of the ball is liable to carry it out of the court). Remember to hit up and over the top of the ball (with wrist) at contact.

SCISSOR KICK OVERHEAD

1. When fading back to reply to a lob with an overhead smash, the right foot should lead back first (from the facing the net volley position).

2. As the right foot leads your left side faces the net and you slide shuffle (side on to the net) behind the falling lob.

3. At execution as you snap wrist (knuckles skyward guaranteeing snap) your right leg should kick forward giving swing momentum, power, and body balance (called the scissor kick). Try it!

DON'T HOG OVERHEAD

1. Player executing has drifted into partner's court to play the overhead. This is not correct.

2. Poacher had better put ball away or he will be passed on the forehand side on the return.

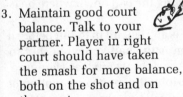

3. Maintain good court balance. Talk to your partner. Player in right court should have taken the smash for more balance, both on the shot and on the court.

THE VOLLEYS AND NET PLAY

The commanding position on the tennis court is at the net. This applies not only to doubles, but also singles.

A volley can be defined as "catching the pace of your opponent's shot and laying the ball down where he is not."

Generally, the volley is any ball hit in the air before it bounces. The exception is the half-volley—a shot to use when the ball bounces right at your feet. Here are a number of panels describing the punching motion of the volley, and the elimination of backswing. Pay attention to the word-pictures emphasizing no backswing; practice them diligently.

A consistent question on the teaching court is, "Can I change to a backhand grip on the volley?" The answer is yes, whenever you have time; otherwise volley with a Continental (service grip) off both forehand and backhand.

Do not allow yourself to develop the "inverted U" or

116

"ward off the storm" backhand volley, whereby you hit the backhand volley with a forehand grip, with your racquet head pointing down and your elbow pointing at the ball. This technique is okay for beginners, but will be very limiting later on.

Women should pay particular attention to the rules in this chapter. I find that, for some reason, women especially tend to resist learning the correct backhand volley.

The half-volley, in my opinion, is one of the most important and difficult shots in the game of tennis, yet it is among the least practiced. Set the ball machine or partner to hit balls right at your feet, and practice your half-volleys until your patience is wearing thin. It will be worth the effort.

For the most part, the half-volley is hit at mid-court while you are trying to approach the net, particularly after your serve. On occasion, it will be necessary to half-volley from the baseline when a swift shot is hit right at your feet. The degree of difficulty of this shot is high. The shot can be made, but to use it as an offensive tactic is inadvisable.

There are definite techniques and word-pictures that must be followed on this shot. Scrutinize these panels closely. Know the "click-click trick" (found in this chapter) and others.

Know when, where, and how to approach and attack the net. Do not be foolish and run to the net on any shot just to practice your volley. This will only force rushed bad habits on your volleying technique. There are two important times to take the net: after hitting a forcing shot deep into a corner or right at your apponent's stomach, or when you force your opponent to hit a short shot (falling into your forecourt).

117

Capitalize on these situations every time.

Practice your standing volleys until you can hit them solidly, deeply, accurately, and consistently before trying to execute volleys on the move.

READY TO VOLLEY

1. This player is ready to volley:
   - Feet are at shoulder width for balance.
   - Racquet head is above wrist.
   - Racquet is in center of body (to go to either side).
   - Eyes are forward, ready to lock onto ball.

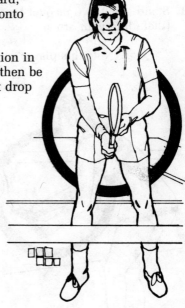

2. Practice this position in backcourt. It will then be habit at net. Don't drop racquet head!

WHERE TO VOLLEY

1. This question often comes up on the teaching court: How far should I be from the net for the volley?

2. Do not crowd the net (opponents easily lob over you). Do not stay too far back (opponents easily hit to your feet, forcing you to volley up defensively).

3. Stand about two racquet lengths from the net (including your arms).

4. Note this player's knees are comfortably bent, arms extended, racquet in center of body. All are correct.

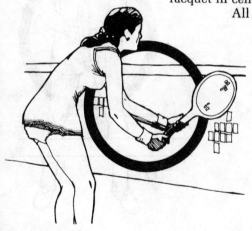

READY TO VOLLEY

1. Player at left is not properly ready to volley. He'll waste valuable time getting racquet into position.

2. When volleying, remember:
   A. Ball comes much faster than bounced ball.
   B. You have less time and distance to judge ball.
   C. Racquet head should be poised to go to either side equally.
   D. You have only half the court to hit to (as opposed to backcourt groundstroke).
   E. Racquet head should be above wrist for firm grip when blocking fast-hit ball.

3. Understand now why player at left is ill-prepared, player at right is ready?

VOLLEY BACKSWING

1. Paramount volleying error is too much backswing.

2. Practice backswing as if there were a brick wall behind you.

3. Volleys are taken in the air. Ball is coming at you half again faster than a ball on the bounce.

4. You have only half the time to react and judge.

5. The shorter the backswing, the better chance for solid impact on the sweet spot.

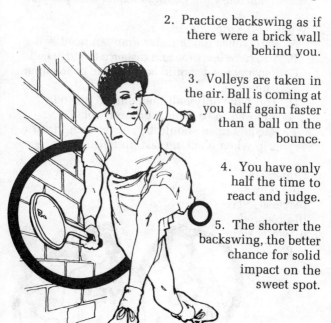

FENCE VOLLEY BACKSWING

1. When at net picture a fence pressed against your back. The volley backswing can only go so far back before hitting the fence.

2. This corrects tendency to swing too far back, thus not having enough time to block the ball in front of body.

3. Do not break wrists at completion of half backswing. No wrist snap and do not drop racquet head. Wrist snap will cause you to "slap" or "swat" weakly at the ball. Keep wrist firm.

4. Volley in front of body for good eye and ball contact.

STEERING WHEEL VOLLEY

1. Having trouble directing the ball where you want it? Volley weak?
   Wrist feel weak?
   Having trouble
   hitting the ball in
   the center of the
   strings?

2. Grab edges of
   racquet face like a
   steering wheel.
   Practice repeated
   shots against a ball
   machine or friend.

3. "Steer" the racquet face up, down, sideways etc.
   Soon you will understand how racquet face directs
   ball. The two hands will make the shot "solid" and
   increase your confidence in the one handed volley.

VOLLEY CONTACT

1. Mis-hits are the nemesis of the volley.

2. Help eye-to-racquet-to-ball contact with this drill:
   Try turning racquet upside down and volleying
   with the grip.

3. Practice this exercise against the ball machine.
   Turn the racquet properly again and watch how
   many more you get on the sweet spot.

10 O'CLOCK VOLLEY

1. Try cocking wrist and racquet head at 10 on the clockface. Note how firm wrist is. Firm wrist will add power.

2. Drop your racquet head to 8 o'clock. Note how loose wrist is. Force of ball will jar racquet face instead of racquet face moving the ball.

3. If the ball is low keep the 10 o'clock position. Drop knees, not racquet head.

BLANKET SPANK VOLLEY

1. Generally, volleys are punched, popped, spanked.

2. Imagine spanking dust out of an old blanket on a line. This will help stop excessive racquet follow-through, and long errors.

3. Squeeze grip until you feel your fingertips. This firms wrist, makes shot more solid.

4. As illustrated, racquet head above wrist guarantees firm wrist.

KARATE CHOP

1. Volleys should be struck from high to low in relation to the level of the ball—a chop, chip or karate punch.

2. Exceptions: Extremely high balls, or at your feet.

3. Don't exaggerate degree of chop. Punch through ball for depth—apply slight chop for backspin to help control and bring confusion to opponent. Backspin makes ball slide low.

PUNCH YOUR VOLLEY

1. Unlike a groundstroke, don't backswing or foreswing. Punch it!

2. When at net: Collect the pace on your opponent's shot, lay the ball where he isn't. Don't try to outhit the hit.

3. Like a boxer, punch racquet head away from your body.

4. Punching improves control, accuracy, consistency—these give command at net.

CATCH BALL IN POCKET

1. Learn a good volley by simply pretending you are catching the ball in the pocket of a baseball glove.

2. Let the strings do the work. This mental image will help you collect the ball in the center of your strings (sweet spot). Catch the ball early.

3. Just as the ball hits the imaginary glove, lock your wrist! Freeze your glove.
   Watch how solid your volley becomes.

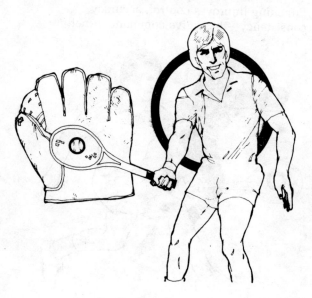

ICE PICK VOLLEY

1. Several words help visualize the volley motion. "Stabbing" or "sticking" the ball on the end of an ice pick are good ones.

2. This player is hurried. Otherwise, his racquet head would be above the wrist and his eyes closer to the ball.

3. Just as you are sticking the ball, squeeze the grip to guarantee firmness.

4. The ice pick image will help improve eye contact.

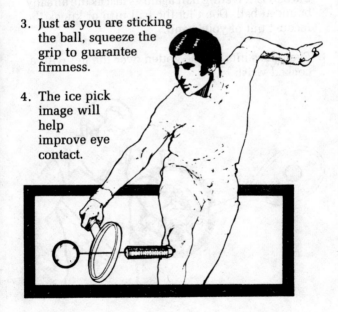

LOCK WRIST AND FOREARM

1. On volley a locked wrist is imperative. The idea on the volley is to catch the pace on your opponent's shot, and let the trampoline effect of the strings do the work for you.

2. Remember: When taking the ball before the bounce, the ball is traveling half again as fast as the already bounced ball. Don't let the ball turn or knock the racquet out of your hand.

3. Even miss-hits can be gotten over the net with a cocked wrist.

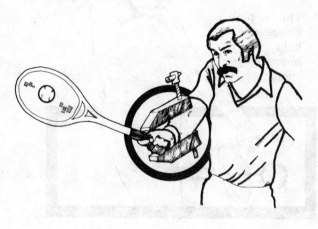

NO JUMP VOLLEYS

1. When volley is chest high or lower, players tend to "help" ball over net by jumping, stiffening or standing up with the shot.

2. Note this airborne player: racquet head is below the wrist, knees are too straight. Eyes are too far from the ball for good perspective and excess movement further impairs vision.

3. Player should bend at knees and play ball over net with angle of racquet face—<u>not</u> his body jump.

V-SHAPED VOLLEY

1. Picture this V to help punch volley with right alignment of arm and racquet head.

2. V Also guarantees a firm wrist for solid impact.

3. Don't waver on follow-through. At impact, lock wrist and freeze. Pose like a statue, check V formation after ball leaves racquet.

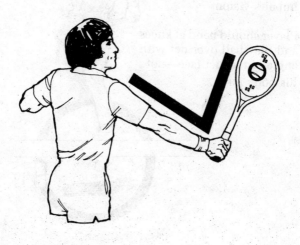

THE 2:30 VOLLEY

1. Keep clockface image in mind when executing backhand volley.

2. The 2 o'clock or 2:30 racquet head position assures a firm wrist—thus solid contact.

3. For lower volleys at 4 or 5 o'clock, drop your knees, not racquet.

4. Dropping racquet head to 4 or 5 will loosen wrist, and cause "golfing," or elevating, or slicing.

FRAME YOUR VOLLEY

1. Do not try to skim your volley too close to the tape. Leave a margin for error.

2. Keep in mind images such as volleying through a window frame (note the center of mental frame is comfortably above the tape level).

3. Hit volleys to opponent service line (middle line) or deeper. Go for depth, accuracy and consistency—power will then come naturally.

RAZOR A LOW VOLLEY

1. Keep racquet face open (tilted up). Imagine knifing that low volley.

2. Imagine shaving the fuzz off lower back of ball with a straight razor.

3. Make sure angle of racquet is tilted enough to carry ball over net.

4. Hit with firm wrist, but play low volley for placement, not power. You are volleying up. Do not hit long!

VOLLEY AT FINGERTIPS

1. The most effective volleys are hit in front of the body. Play from behind the ball for better eye contact and good weight shift into the hit.

2. Practice leaving free hand in front of you for better balance. Try hitting no later than when ball is at free hand's fingertips. Meet ball. Don't wait for it to come to you.

3. With racquet face flush to ball, the earlier the hit, the flatter the trajectory into opponent's court. Late hit means popping up.

THE BOWL SHAPED VOLLEY

1. To understand proper racquet face angle on various levels of volleys, visualize a giant bowl.

2. A. If ball is shoulder high or higher close racquet face (turn it slightly downward) like the top of the bowl.
   B. If ball is middle height, keep racquet face flush to the ball (straight up and down).

   C. Racquet face is open for lower balls (slanted slightly up) to scoop balls up and over net like the bottom rim of bowl.

   D. Always keep the image of the bowl in mind when practicing.

VOLLEY EYE CONTACT

1. This player's bent knees bring his eyes close to ball on low forehand volley.

2. Standing straight up is not only physically awkward, it draws eyes away from ball, resulting in lost perspective and "feel."

3. Your eyes are you. If they're too high, so is the rest of you.

4. It's virtually impossible to get down too low—but easy to stand too high.

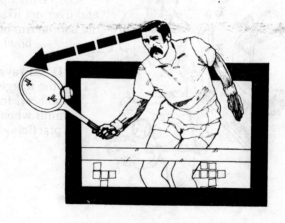

CROSS FOOT VOLLEY

1. The right foot should step toward the left net post (backhand volley); the left foot toward the right net post (forehand volley).

2. Most players (even advanced) don't realize advantages of the cross-foot volley:
   A. Slide is guaranteed to be toward net.
   B. Weight will shift into the ball and toward net.
   C. You will pick ball off high and early.

THE STOP VOLLEY

1. What is a stop volley? What's the objective? To stop
   ball short in opponent's forecourt when he is
   running in backcourt.

2. Go at it as if you were going to drive volley; instead,
   soften your grip at impact, stop your racquet face
   (almost draw it back after contact). Do not follow
   through!

3. This is a good practice
   measure for all volleys,
   since a common error is to
   swing on the volley.

AVOID HALF VOLLEY FROM BASELINE

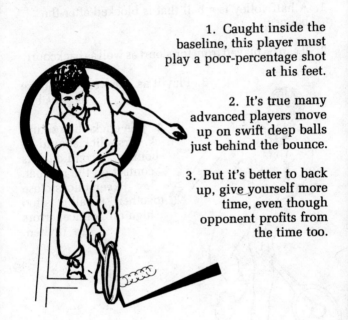

1. Caught inside the baseline, this player must play a poor-percentage shot at his feet.

2. It's true many advanced players move up on swift deep balls just behind the bounce.

3. But it's better to back up, give yourself more time, even though opponent profits from the time too.

143

CLICK-CLICK TRICK

1. A half volley is a ball that is blocked after the bounce.

2. It can be played from forecourt as well as backcourt.

3. Play it as close to the bounce as possible.

4. Use click-click sound trick. First click should be bounce. Second click is contact on the racquet. Keep clicks close together—if ball gets too high off bounce, errors are invited.

CLICK   CLICK

WRIST HALF VOLLEY WHEN LATE

1. The ball has gotten behind the player. He is using wrist to get the racquet face looking toward net (keep wrist firm).

2. The racquet face is quite flush to the ball.

3. He will move top edge of racquet head a little forward (closed racquet face) to counteract ball's tendency to reflect off racquet face upward. This trick will keep the volley from going too deep.

LOB VOLLEY

1. The lob volley is definitely an offensive shot (meaning if you get it over opponent's head it's usually a winner).

2. There is a big chance for error. It's used when all four players are at net, utilizing surprise.

3. Play this shot by the score: if you're ahead, try it!

4. The shot is a volley with the racquet face slanted with a sharp angle up.

KEEP WRIST UP

1. Practice "freezing" finished position on the volley with racquet up. Have a friend or ball machine hit balls to your volley-punch, then check racquet head.

2. Both players have volleyed a ball about waist high. The player on left incorrectly dropped his racquet head which will result in errors sliced wide into the net or golfed long. His shot will be weak due to a loose wrist.

3. Player on right has volleyed solidly and accurately due to a firm wrist guaranteed by racquet head up.

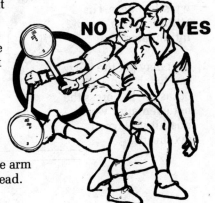

4. Finish with a "V" formed between whole arm and racquet head.

TENACIOUS ATTACK

1. When at net, or after an overhead smash, attack the net with a ferociously positive attitude, no matter how weak your shot is.

2. Once you're this close in to net, retreating is not feasible.

3. This player looks like he's ready to wrestle a bear. His attitude alone intimidates.

4. You may get the "fuzz sandwich" on occasion, but press the net even after weak mis-hit volleys or overheads.

EQUIPMENT, CONDITIONING, TACTICS, STRATEGY, MENTAL PREPARATION

These topics are what I call the auxiliary elements of a well-rounded tennis game. They give supplementary assistance to a good stroke foundation. An advanced tennis game cannot be developed without a sound knowledge of each.

"You are only as good as your equipment" is an old—and true—adage. In tennis, poor equipment can be very restricting and can lead to injuries under given conditions. For example, a sprung or weak racquet frame can cause vibrations that travel to a person's arm, resulting in tennis elbow. Poor arches in tennis shoes can lead to foot injuries. It pays for a player to constantly watch consumer guides for quality equipment. There are excellent unbiased articles in many industry and trade periodicals and in the major tennis magazines found at any well-supplied newsstand. Recently, there have been some excellent books published dealing exclusively with equipment.

149

Check your bookstores. I am a great believer in using the finest equipment.

There are also many books on conditioning. In the last five years there has been a movement toward physical fitness and conditioning, including diet, exercise, etc. I am a firm believer in all of it. I would recommend as much conditioning as a player's time, money, and stamina allow. If you can get help from a professional trainer, all the better.

Remember the old maxim, "Condition the body and the heart and mind follow." In a tennis player's world, the psychology of being fit is crucial to a positive winning attitude. When a player is out of condition for a match he is like a bird with one wing. He is psychologically deficient when "the flags go up and the gun goes off" on tournament day. Running is the best all-around conditioner for tennis. Do it, and have a winning posture when you shake hands at the net.

Obviously, physical and mental preparation are related. As the axiom goes, "Tennis is 65 percent mental and 35 percent physical." This may not be totally true, but it comes very close. There is never a winner who cannot control his temperament. He can turn anger into an aggressive, winning disposition. Remember: It is only a loser who gives in to emotion on the court. Pay attention to the subtleties hidden in the headings and text of this book that concern mental attitudes, preparation, targets, images, strategies, and tactics. Learn to understand the difference between positive and negative thinking. After all, if you are concentrating on a positive mental word-picture while executing a shot, it takes your mind off the negative—such as, "My gosh, what if I miss this shot?"

Thinking positively brings you into the world of

tactics and strategy. In this text I have used copy and line drawings to put together the most important and popularly used tactics and strategies. They are a great beginning to your arsenal of fun maneuvering on the tennis court. "The Tarzans end up defeated and the thinkers end up lining their trophy cabinets with the hardware." Tennis can truly be a David and Goliath story. Know your theories—the center theory of no angle of return, the corner theory, the angle percentages. Know what it means to hit to an opponent's strength to get to his weakness, or not to open up your own court. Tennis is a thinking man's game. Think, and continue your winning ways!

WHAT ABOUT STRINGING?

1. Go to your pro! Next best, go to the best pro shop or sporting goods store. Ask for the top tennis person, not just a sales clerk.

2. Average string tension in a wooden racquet is 55 to 60 pounds.

3. The tighter the strings the more power but less control (ball leaves strings faster). The looser the strings the more control, less power (ball stays on strings longer).

4. I advocate tight strings only for advanced players. Always go for control before power.

WHAT EQUIPMENT IS NECESSARY TO A GOOD FOREHAND? IS EQUIPMENT A GIMMICK?

1. Note the player here has:
   A. Wrapped his grip in gauze to absorb the perspiration of his hand on the grip. No slippage.

   B. He is using a resin bag like a baseball pitcher does; he keeps it in the back pocket of his shorts. This is another method of keeping your playing hand dry.

   C. The player uses a wristband to keep the perspiration from running down onto his hand.

   D. The headband keeps perspiration out of the eyes and keeps the hair from bothering the player. I advocate using all these methods.

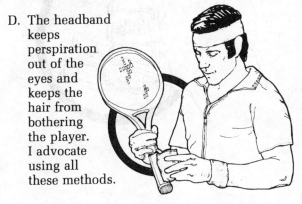

153

GRIP SLIPPING?

1. Clean with alcohol, water, soap (saddlesoap if leather) and toothbrush to get into cracks.

2. Clean often. Toxic elements in perspiration corrode good leather.

3. Wear wrist band to cut perspiration from arm.

4. Keep a resin bag in your pocket. Don't be afraid to use it.

5. During play, rub wet grip on fence wire to roughen for better hold.

VIDEO TAPE

1. A picture tells a thousand words. Tennis instruction has advanced 100 percent in the last 15 years due to visual aids.

2. Treat yourself to a tennis camp. Look at your game stroke by stroke, in slow motion, fast motion, and playback replay.

3. If you are already spending money on lessons, then add this dimension of instruction. The finest players in the world do. So should you.

USE TEACHING AIDS TO IMPROVE YOUR FOREHAND TENNIS STROKE

There are several ways to practice tennis. One of the ways is with teaching aids.

This player is practicing and "grooving" a good forehand stroke against this teaching aid. She can practice her position, footwork, and stroke against this standing target.

Practicing in this manner is the same as a baseball player swinging without being pitched to, a golfer practicing his swing without a ball on the tee, or a boxer "shadow boxing" without an opponent.

The best athletes do it! Why not try it for tennis? In a short time, a good swing will be natural to you.

USE "MIRROR TENNIS" AS A PRACTICE METHOD FOR YOUR FOREHAND

1. As a "Teaching Pro" I will many times be asked by students, "How can I practice what I have learned in my lessons?"

2. In my opinion, there are five forms of practice that are meaningful.

   1. Ball Machines
   2. Backboards
   3. Rallying with another person
   4. Teaching Aids
   5. Practicing opposite a mirror, particularly for beginners

3. Remember this line: "For every 10 balls in the court in practice, three will be in during a match."

BALL MACHINE VOLLEY

1. Practice on the ball machine. It's one of the finest teaching aids, great for volley practice.

2. Ball machines can do almost anything a player can. It is controlled practice! The only other kinds of practice are with other players or against the backboard (not always controlled).

3. You can isolate and combat weaknesses with a ball machine. You can hit many balls in a short period as opposed to rallying. It strengthens your wrist.

4. Set the machine for the half volley (balls bouncing at your feet) and hit hundreds. The half volley is one of the most difficult shots, and the least practiced.

V UPS FOR STOMACH

1. Lie flat on your back. Sit up, forming a V between your toes and your shoulders. Try to touch your toes without bending your knees.

2. This exercise is excellent for tennis players. It strengthens the stomach, groin, and seat muscles, all of which can be easily injured in a sudden move on the court.

3. Always take time to warm up and do stretch exercises no matter how good you feel your condition is.

USE ISOMETRIC EXCERCISES TO STRENGTHEN YOUR HAND, FOREARM, FINGERS AND GRIP

1. Put both hands together, intermingling the fingers. Clasp the hands together.

2. Squeeze the fingers together repeatedly. Make one hand resist the squeeze of the other. Press the palms together and apart to strengthen the wrist and forearm.

3. Conditioning your arm will help to avoid Tennis Elbow or Tendonitis in the fingers or wrist.

STRENGTHENING GRIP

1. Use a fat rubber band. Stretch with thumb and small finger. Make a fist, then repeat.

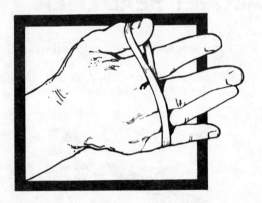

2. This is good for the wrist and forearm too.

3. Conditioning is as important as practice. This helps avoid tendonitis and "tennis elbow."

AVOID TENNIS ELBOW ON THE FOREHAND! DO NOT "TWIST" OR "FLIP" YOUR RACQUET HEAD OVER

1. When the weight of the racquet head with all of its momentum is flipped or twisted over, the result can be a definite strain on the tendon that connects to the bone (Epicondyle) of the elbow.

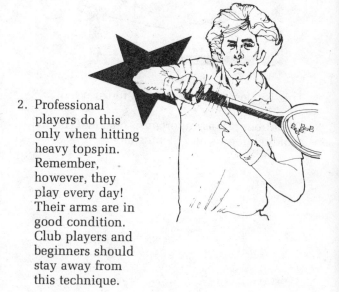

2. Professional players do this only when hitting heavy topspin. Remember, however, they play every day! Their arms are in good condition. Club players and beginners should stay away from this technique.

PROPER WEIGHT EXERCISES CAN PREVENT TENNIS ELBOW

1. Two major causes of tennis elbow are:

   a. Improper stroking,

   b. Poor muscle strength.

2. Use a 3- to 4-pound dumbbell or even a household iron. Place arm on a table, palm downward.

Use wrist to lift, and hold several seconds. Lower weight. Repeat 10 times. Use more weight as arm gets stronger.

LOWER BACK PROBLEMS? SOME EXERCISES TO EASE THEM

A. This exercise stretches the lower back and warms up the groin and the hamstring muscles of the upper leg. Take the illustrated position and repeatedly reach for the toes. Switch to other leg and repeat.

B. This warms up the lower back. Lie stomach down, with arms pushing chest up. Arch lower back. Move head slowly in circles to warm neck and upper back.

CAN WEIGHT LIFTING STRENGTHEN YOUR STROKES?

Yes, but know what you are doing. Never try to build just bulk. Use light weights and repetition to build tone, not thick muscles. Consult a professional weight lifting trainer.

IS JOGGING GOOD FOR TENNIS?

1. Yes! It strengthens feet, legs, stamina and endurance. But use caution:

2. Be wary of hard surfaces—this can be rough on a tennis player's lower back. Try to run in sand or other soft surfaces.

3. Don't jog in tennis shoes. Get good running shoes with arch supports and builtup cushioned heels and soles.

4. Consult a trainer or doctor. Build pace and distance slowly. Don't overdo it.

THE DROP SHOT

1. This is a touch shot usually used when you are in command and opponents on the defensive in the backcourt.

2. Lighten up your grip, spoon racquet face as you cushion ball on the strings and touch it barely over the net. Shorten follow-through.

3. Good tactic against opponents who do not like to come forward, or are weak at the net. Bring them forward, then punish with a lob or drive.

4. Know when, where and how to use this shot. Generally used when ahead.

DIAGONAL NET ATTACK

1. When moving to forehand or backhand volleys, do so diagonally. Why?

   A. You cut ball off early, keeping opponent off balance.
   B. The earlier you pick ball out of the air, the flatter (lower) your shot will be.
   C. You will hit ball at a higher point above the net (offensive volley). If the ball drops below the tape you are now volleying up (defensive volley).

MOVE IN ON 2ND SERVE

1. This intimidating tactic puts the pressure on the server. Make him thread the needle.

2. Why move in on 2nd serve?
   A. The serve is not as hard and has spin.
   B. A spinning ball curves or kicks. Move in on it before it (the angle) gets away from you.
   C. The commanding position is the net (this gives you a chance to gain a couple of steps in).

3. Only move in far enough to where you are not rushed. Get set before service motion is started.

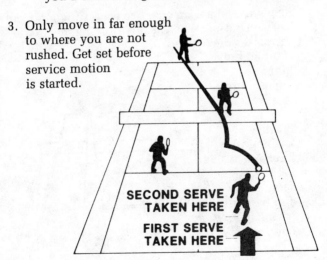

SECOND SERVE TAKEN HERE

FIRST SERVE TAKEN HERE

HIT YOUR FOREHAND WITH DEPTH! PRACTICE WITH A MENTAL IMAGE OF THE SHADED COURT

1. The commanding position on the court is at the net! Keep your opponent away from the forecourt with deep, "probing" shots.

2. Remember, there are only two ways your opponent can gain the net: When he hits a forcing shot to you, then takes the net and when you involuntarily hit short and give him an opportunity to advance.

3. Practice keeping your forehand between the service line and baseline on the first bounce.

HAVING TROUBLE HITTING THE "DOWN-THE-LINE" FOREHAND? TRY USING THE "TILTED COURT" MENTAL IMAGE!

1. Almost any player can hit the cross-court shot easier than the down-the-line, simply because it is seventeen feet farther cross-court. There is more court to hit into.

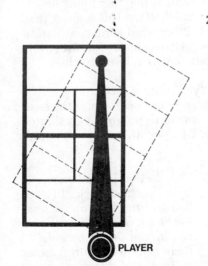

PLAYER

2. Try tilting the court mentally (such as the dotted court), then pretend you're hitting to the cross-court corner. This practice exercise will help you turn, increase your confidence, and "groove" your down-the-line shot.

171

ARE YOU PLAYING SMART TENNIS? USE THE "TRAFFIC LIGHT" MENTAL IMAGE WHEN PLAYING YOUR FOREHAND FROM YOUR OWN COURT! PLAY BETTER PERCENTAGE TENNIS!

1. This section of the court is the "red light" or "danger area" particularly if the ball is lower than tape height. If the ball is played hard, considering the angle needed to get it over the net, an error over the baseline is likely to occur. Use "touch!"

2. This section is the "yellow light" or "caution area". The distance between your position and the error over the baseline is becoming progressively shorter. If the ball is below tape height, use "placement," not power.

3. This section is the "green light" or "safety area". In other words, from here on back is the "back court" area and you can hit out safely, because there is a lot of court between yourself and the error beyond the baseline.

USE IMAGINARY "NET ON THE NET" FOR FOREHAND DEPTH AND SAFETY

1. Players too often try to skim a shot too close to the net tape, resulting in hitting into the net or at best shallow bouncers.

2. Use the mental image of a second net atop the real one in practice. It'll improve steadiness and give greater depth.

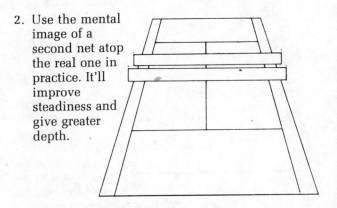

3. Mental tactics such as this will also take your mind off the possible error.

WHEN SHOULD YOU GET YOUR RACQUET BACK? ARE YOU REACTING SOON ENOUGH?

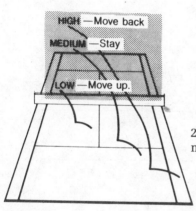

HIGH —Move back

MEDIUM —Stay

LOW —Move up.

1. Get your racquet back when you see if the shot is coming to forehand or backhand. Determine direction by the time the ball clears the net.

2. If the ball is high, move back, as it will bounce deep. Move forward for the low bouncer, and hit it at the apex of the bounce. The medium ball will come to you; stay where you are.

3. Move before the ball bounces; play it, or it'll play you.

PLAY FOREHAND WITH A SAFETY MARGIN. PLAY THE "COURT WITHIN A COURT"

1. Notice the shaded court within the regular singles court. Play in there.

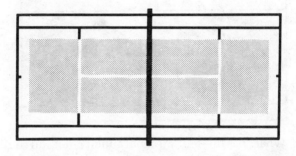

2. Only touring pros "hit for the lines." Intermediate and club players make needless errors aiming for the lines.

3. Playing the "court within the court" usually results in close to the line shots anyway. Steadiness is the top priority.

THE HOURGLASS THEORY

1. As with all sports, it's smart to play tennis percentages.

2. Statistics show that almost 80 percent of oncoming shots fall within the "hourglass" area.

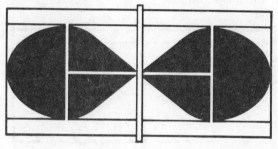

3. What does this tell you about anticipation and court position?

4. Don't get caught standing in the hourglass. Exceptions: When volleying; when stationed there in doubles.

5. Standing in the hourglass means being rushed, digging balls up at your feet.

BEWARE OF BACKSPIN

1. The dark arrow is topspin, the dotted arrow underspin on a given hit.

2. Forehand crosscourt demands topspin 90 percent of the time. Why?

   a. Topspin can clear net higher and still stay in.
   b. More velocity.
   c. Wider bounce.

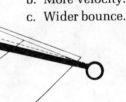

3. Save backspin (underspin) when trying to confuse or defend. Backspin floats and bounces high, giving opponent more time to get to ball.

HITTING EARLY OR LATE? MAKE RACQUET "LOOK" AT TARGET

1. Ball will go where the racquet face "looks."

2. For cross-court, swing sooner, but not necessarily faster.

3. For down the line, swing later, but not slower.

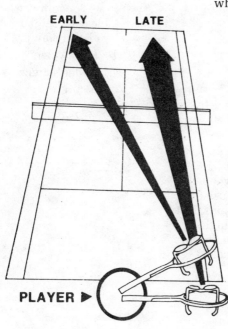

EARLY   LATE

PLAYER ▶

CROSSCOURT OR DOWN THE LINE?

1. Crosscourt is always a better percentage shot than down the line. There are 17 more feet of court from corner to corner, and the net is 4 to 6 inches lower at the center.

2. Don't dismiss down the line shots. They're handy. With time you'll come to pick which you want at will.

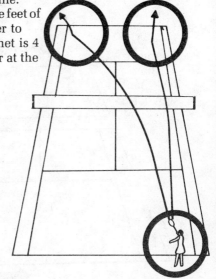

FOREHAND DEFENSIVE LOB

1. Use it when opponent commands net, and is running you back and forth. You're in trouble.

2. Push up a high lob, giving you time to get back to the center of the court.

3. Lob crosscourt: you have 17 more feet than down the line.

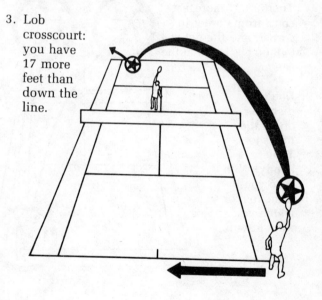

SOFT SERVE THROWING YOU?

1. Be patient. Hit deep to shaded targets. Don't overhit.

2. Move in. Cut off the angle of the serve. Then move up to command the net.

3. Keep the pressure on with placement and steadiness.

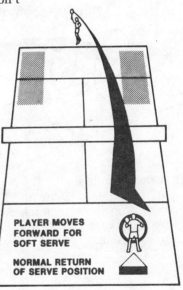

PLAYER MOVES FORWARD FOR SOFT SERVE

NORMAL RETURN OF SERVE POSITION

LOB TO BEAT SOFTBALLERS AND PUSHERS

1. Softballers win on your errors. They are maddeningly steady. They never give you pace to play off.

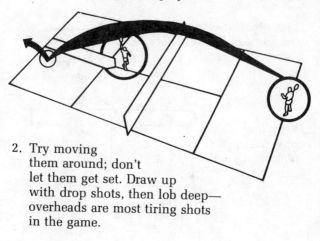

2. Try moving them around; don't let them get set. Draw up with drop shots, then lob deep— overheads are most tiring shots in the game.

"SHORT ANGLE" SERVE RETURN

1. Most players are comfortable returning wide forehands deep down the line.

2. But hitting the "short angle" moves opponent sideways and forward. Short angle forces opponent to hit up, and you can capitalize on this.

3. This gives variety, unpredictability to your returns.

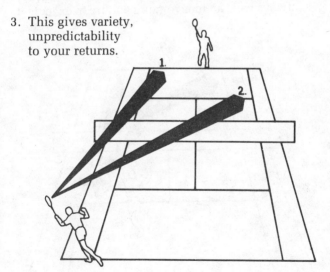

GO FOR THE CORNERS

1. Hit where opponent isn't—to the corners. Keep him moving.

2. In practice rallying, avoid always hitting down the middle. Always pick a target—a corner—and practice hitting to it.

3. When warming up, don't put the ball away but always have an idea in mind and try to execute it.

THE OFFENSIVE LOB

1. Use it only when ahead, and as a surprise. Often it makes a handy putaway shot.

2. Margin of error is large—could result in overhead smash if hit too low.

3. Hit so it just clears opponent's racquet; you can go to the net on this.

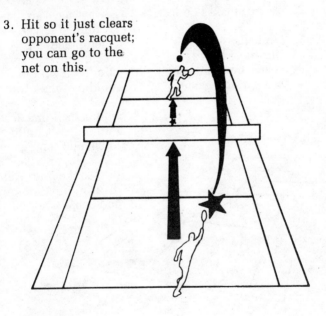

IMPROVE YOUR FOREHAND WITH DRILLS! PRACTICE THE CROSSCOURT FOREHAND TO FOREHAND PATTERN

1. Practice makes perfect.

2. Ten balls in the court in practice means three balls in the court in a game.

3. Always have an idea in mind, a target, when practicing. Avoid rallying blindly down the middle of the court.

4. In this drill practice hitting forehand to forehand keeping the ball "deeper" than the service line. This drill improves depth and consistency.

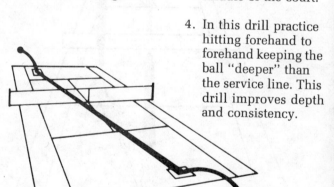

WHAT ARE SOME ADVANTAGES OF TOPSPIN ON THE FOREHAND SIDE?

1. The ball can be hit higher than usual over the net. The applied overspin will aerodynamically help the ball drop deep into the court. Something other than gravity is helping the ball drop into the court. The force of air is greater on top of the ball as it travels over the net due to the overspin.

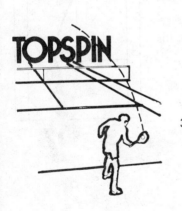

2. The ball bites the opponent's court and jumps at him and takes a sudden acceleration due to the spin. The ball bounds high, making it difficult to handle.

3. Warning! Keep your topspin shots deep unless your opponent is taking the net. Short hit topspin is a setup.

PULL FOE OFF COURT

1. Practice wide, flat or slice serve to forehand court. Simple, but effective.

2. Foe must scramble defensively. You move to net, intercept his awkward return and volley at will—either far to his backhand, or slip it behind him if he anticipates that.

3. Don't send serve out for grabs. Always have a plan.

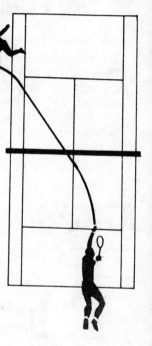

KNOW THE TOUGH TRIO

1. Don't be imprisoned by one serve. Your opponent will soon get wise to it.

2. Learn to keep him off balance with variety.

3. Twist, flat (topspin), slice—these three serves should be in your arsenal.

4. Probe and exploit with deep, penetrating deliveries.

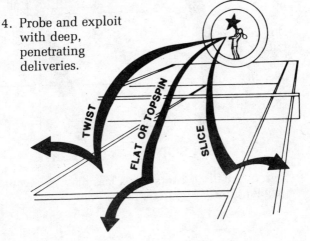

FLAT AND SPIN: THE DIFFERENCE

1. Flat serve travels faster, but lower. More chance for error.

2. Spin serve is slower but arcs high over net and curves to left. Less chance of error.

SPIN SERVE

FLAT SERVE

3. Spin is usually a 2nd serve. Class players have it. Develop it!

CORRECT PLACEMENTS

1. Don't always serve to the shaded areas. Serve will be too shallow.

2. Practice probing serves deep to the corners of service court.

3. Firing right at opponent will cramp his return.

4. Practice consistency, accuracy and depth. Power is the lowest priority, unless a Pro player.

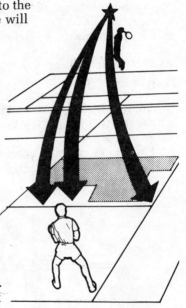

SMASH TO MIDDLE

1. The biggest target on the overhead smash in doubles is down the middle. This causes confusion for opponents as to who should take the ball.

2. This tactic will employ "The Center Theory of No Angle of Return," meaning that opponents will likely hit back down middle (it's difficult to hit crosscourt or down the line from middle). Your partner will be looking to cut the volley off.

3. There is more court to hit into down the middle. You're taking a bigger chance going to the corners.

ELEMENT OF CONFUSION

1. An excellent tactic is to play the middle in doubles, particularly when in trouble. Consider:
   A. The net is four to six inches lower in the middle than sides.
   B. There is more court to hit into than down the line (distance in footage).
   C. There will be an element of confusion on the opponents' part as to who should take the ball.

2. When in drastic trouble, lob or hit down the middle.

ROPE YOUR DOUBLES STRATEGY

1. Move together! When left player moves right player closes any gaps.

2. Pretend you are roped to your doubles partner. Move in together, move sideways together.

3. Try not to move back together unless there is a sure kill of a weak overhead on opponents' part. Try to keep one player at the net as an "ace in the hole."

USE "MENTAL TARGETS" WHEN HITTING YOUR FOREHAND CROSSCOURT

1. Note: the player hit the ball "early" in front of the body like addressing the ball in front of the plate in baseball.

2. The shoulders have opened up well and the racquet follows through a little higher and further than usual.

3. Using "mental targets" in practice, and playing takes your mind off the error and avoids the negative thought process of the possible error. This relates to the power of positive thinking, hitting the ball from one ordinate point to another.

195

"FEATHER" THAT FOREHAND LOB. "PUSH" THE SHOT. AVOID "HITTING" IT

1. This player is in trouble. He is reaching, hitting off the wrong foot; moreover, the ball is in "bad" position. It is not in the "strike zone" (chest to knee high). The player is wisely lobbing the ball. He is "defending" instead of "offending". Note the racquet face is looking up.

2. Use "touch" when lobbing. Avoid "jerking" or "hitting". Refrain from any sudden moves during the shot. Slow down your racquet head. "Push" the ball with a high follow-through. Incorporate a whole arm "sweeping motion".

COMMUNICATE IN DOUBLES

1. These players are caught incorrectly in "line" or in the middle formation. The big question is: who's calling signals?

2. Answer: Both players should talk when necessary. Generally, the player in back can see the whole court and direct most of the traffic. Use brief expressions such as "Let it bounce," "Switch," "Stay," "Move in."

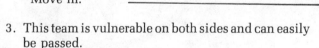

3. This team is vulnerable on both sides and can easily be passed.

WHO PLAYS MIDDLE?

1. The age-old question in doubles. Both are right-handed. Player on the right should hit forehand volley.

2. But player on right has been caught not ready. His partner had to come over to play a backhand volley and lose court position.

3. Maintain good court balance for winning doubles.

STARE 'EM DOWN

1. When ready to serve, take advantage of break in the action. Take a deep breath. Keep foe waiting. Make him edgy.

2. Set up mental target. Note by opponent's position where return is likely to come.

3. Be aware of where you are going to put the ball on your toss.

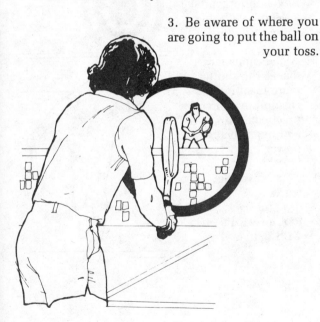

ALWAYS SERVE FOR A TARGET

1. Before beginning, have a plan. Then try to execute it.

2. Envision target, take a deep breath then serve through it.

3. A conscious target makes the shot more meaningful. Discipline yourself: practice accuracy and depth before power.

4. This player has correctly brought back foot forward with delivery.

DON'T LET THE WEATHER PSYCH YOU

1. The sophisticated player isn't bothered by weather variations. He stays mentally tough, realizing the opponent faces the same conditions.

2. Never let opponent know the weather is bothering you. Your frustration will only inspire him. Act like it's your kind of day.

DON'T MONKEY AROUND

1. Any time you spend acting cute or messing around hurts your own concentration.

2. With few exceptions, the real champions show good demeanor on court. Watch Evert, Borg, Vilas and Orantes for examples of solid concentration.

3. Let the score show your winning ability, and be humble. To be a winner, it helps to act like one.

202

SAVE PRAYING FOR CHURCH

1. Hit important shots relaxed. Concentrate on the ball, net and court.

2. Stress causes a tightening up. The player hits stiffly, with too many muscles tensed. In short, he "chokes," then tries to "pray the shot in."

3. Praying helps, but usually before and after the match. In action, learn to relax.

203

WATCH THE BALL TO THE RACQUET FACE AND WATCH IT LEAVE FOR BETTER EYE CONCENTRATION

1. When watching the ball correctly, you will see a yellow "blur" of several balls in a row as the racquet meets the ball.

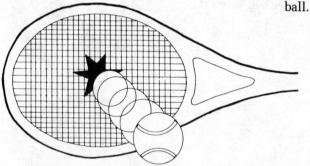

2. This trick will improve your ability to watch the ball and avoid mis-hits. The most common error in tennis is to pull your eyes off the ball and look away from the ball at contact.

LOB SMARTLY

1. When pulled or driven wide to your forehand or backhand corners, don't hit the ball, lob it!

2. Practice the lob endlessly. These players, by properly lobbing, can reverse a totally defensive position to an offensive or equal position by simply getting the ball over the net rusher's head or high into the backcourt.

3. Lobbing gives you time to get back to middle of court. If you hit a ground stroke, it will get to opponent fast and he will simply hit to your open side before you gain balance.

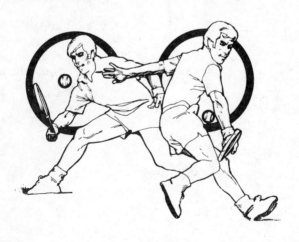

ENCOURAGE PARTNER

1. You must communicate in doubles: for encouragement and for strategy and tactics.

2. Never show disappointment, anger, anxiety.

3. Doubles takes team work, and the strongest type of teamwork is psychological support of your partner. At times your partner will play poorly and you'll be great. Remember! It can be the other way around.

4. It's intimidating to opponents to know your team is together, not apart. Be patient, sympathetic and a winner!

DON'T FONDLE GRIP

1. Advanced players get away with it; all others cannot!

2. Players tend to take a correct grip, then nervously spoil it by taking fingers on and off the racquet while waiting. This results in a large chance of losing the correct grip.

3. Clamp your correct grip on the racquet, check it with your eye, then hold it! Do not remove fingers once grip is set!

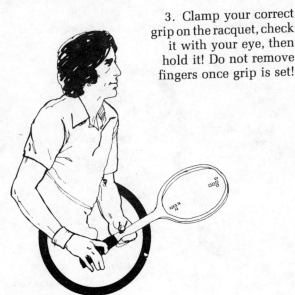

"DOUBLE EYE CONCENTRATION" ON HARD SHOTS

1. When lunging for an important but difficult shot, keep both eyes focused to the point of exaggeration directly on the ball.

2. When the body moves abruptly, the eyes tend to jump or "dance" away from the target.

3. The illustrated player, though desperately lunging, retains this exaggerated double eye concentration.

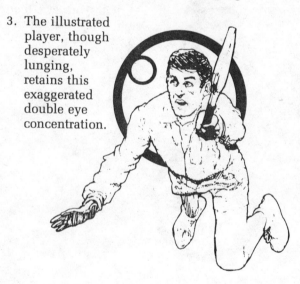

CHARGE! COMMAND THE NET!

1. This player is responding to a short or weakly hit ball.

2. He is sending the shot deep to opponent's corner and is charging the net.

3. This is the commanding position. Make your opponent thread the needle by hitting down the line, crosscourt or over your head. Force errors.

WHEN TO "SURRENDER"

1. Is hustling every ball good? No. Save energy, stamina for important points. Don't chase opponent's sure putaways.

2. Conversely, go all-out on the big points. Hold nothing back.

3. Although he's on his knees, this player is going all-out, hanging in, on a crucial point.

WHEN TO USE FOREHAND DROP SHOT

1. Use it from your own forecourt, or forward of service line.

2. Use it when opponent is pressed deep, and on the move, usually sideways or back.

3. It's your "knuckleball," best used when you're ahead and opponent is pressing; it keeps him off balance.

BEAT OPPONENT TO PUNCH

1. This player is confidently, aggressively taking a low ball on the rise. Like a boxer, his weight is shifting to the front.

2. Remember the basic singles strategy: Getting to the peak of the ball's bounce first, then stroking it down the line or crosscourt, means being in command—beating opponent to the punch.

3. Keep your opponent on the merry-go-round. Keep the ball where he is not by getting the jump on the ball.

"SPOON" THE DROPSHOT

1. Pretend you have a large spoon in your hand. "Cup" the ball in the bowl of the spoon.

2. Hide drop shot: act as if preparing a punishing forehand, but shorten swing, lighten grip, slide racquet face under the ball, gradually "spooning" upward.

3. Feel the ball on the strings; "hold" it there.

WHAT ABOUT THE TWO HANDED FOREHAND? GOOD OR BAD?

1. An advantage of this shot is: it is a secure, confident, steady, deceptive stroke. With this technique, the player can hold the ball on the racquet face longer and change direction at the last moment.

2. This is a shot that has been possessed by some of the World Champions over the past decades. The foremost example is Pancho Segura, now the head teaching pro and Tennis Director at La Costa Resort in Southern California.

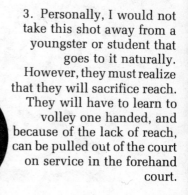

3. Personally, I would not take this shot away from a youngster or student that goes to it naturally. However, they must realize that they will sacrifice reach. They will have to learn to volley one handed, and because of the lack of reach, can be pulled out of the court on service in the forehand court.

4. Do not make the mistake of changing a natural one handed shot to an "educated" two handed.

214

GLOSSARY OF TENNIS TERMS

ACE A serve the receiver is unable to get his racket on.

AD COURT Another name for the left service court, to which the serve is delivered when the score is someone's ad.

AD-IN A scorekeeping term that omits the server's name but indicates that the score is his ad.

AD-OUT A scoring term that indicates the receiver's advantage.

ALLEY The area, four-and-a-half feet wide, added to each side of a singles court.

APPROACH SHOT A running-in shot behind which a player advances to the net.

BACKCOURT The area, eighteen feet deep, between the service line and the base line.

BACKSPIN A rotary motion, applied by undercutting the ball, which makes it spin in the opposite direction of its flight path.

BASE LINE The rear line at each end of the court.

CANNONBALL A flat, powerful serve given maximum speed.

CENTER MARK A mark, four inches long, that shows the midpoint of the base line.

CENTER SERVICE LINE The boundary that divides the forecourt into right and left service courts.

CHIP The same as chop.

CHOP A stroke that gives the ball underspin or backspin.

215

CONTINENTAL GRIP A compromise about halfway between the Eastern forehand and Eastern backhand grips, used by some players to eliminate the necessity of shifting the hand on the racket. It is also known as the service grip because it's the grip most commonly used in serving.

CROSSCOURT SHOT A ball hit diagonally to the opposite side of the court—as opposed to a shot hit down the line, whose flight path is roughly parallel to the side line.

DEUCE COURT Another name for the right service court.

DINK A general term for any kind of shot plopped softly over the net.

DOUBLE FAULT The failure of the server to put either his first or second service into play (which costs him the point).

DOWN-THE-LINE A shot hit roughly parallel to the side line, as opposed to a crosscourt shot.

DRIVE A shot hit with a full stroke, either forehand or backhand, after the bounce.

DROP SHOT A soft stroke hit with backspin that lands just beyond the net.

DROP VOLLEY A drop shot hit off a ball on the fly. Also called a stop volley. It drops short in opponent's forecourt.

EASTERN GRIP The standard "shake hands" tennis grip, which must be rotated for backhand strokes.

FAULT The failure of the server to put his first serve in play.

FLAT Descriptive of a serve given very little spin—and consequently hard for the server to control.

GLOSSARY OF TENNIS TERMS

FOOT FAULT A fault called on a server for stepping on or over the base line before his racquet touches the ball.

FORCING SHOT Any shot with which one player assumes the initiative, forcing his opponent into an error or weak return or putting him in an awkward position.

FORECOURT The area, twenty-one feet deep, between the net and the service line.

THE CEMENT ARM A slang expression meaning to choke up, to get the jitters.

GROUND STROKE Any shot hit after it has bounced, as opposed to a volley, which is hit on the fly.

HALF COURT LINE The line that goes width-wise across the middle of the court, parallel to the baseline.

HALF-VOLLEY Name for a pick-up shot, a ball hit immediately after it bounces.

LOB Any ball lofted high in the air, usually over the head of an opponent.

NO MAN'S LAND The area between the base line and the service line, where lingering is ill-advised.

ONE-UP-AND-ONE-BACK A tandem formation used in playing doubles.

OVERHEAD A ball smashed from a high position off a lob.

OVERSPIN A rotary motion that accentuates the forward movement of the ball, as if it were turning somersaults. Synonymous with topspin.

PACE A desirable combination of speed and momentum. A fast shot with "something on it" is said to carry pace.

217

PLACEMENT Any shot hit out of an opponent's reach.

PUT AWAY To hit a shot so well that no return can be made.

READ To anticipate an opponent's moves accurately, usually with the help of small clues.

RETRIEVER A player who excels at running down and returning hard shots.

SERVE The act of putting the ball into play.

SERVICE BREAK A game in which the server loses.

SERVICE COURT The area in which the serve must land for the ball to be in play.

SERVICE LINE The back boundary of the service courts, twenty-one feet from the net.

SITTER Any shot that hangs invitingly in the air, easy to return for a winner.

SLICE A stroke with heavy sidespin. It breaks to a right-handed player's left.

SMASH An overhead stroke hit forcefully, intended to win the point outright.

STOP VOLLEY A drop shot hit on the fly; a drop volley.

SWEET SPOT The area in the center of the racquet head. A stroke launched from the sweet spot carries maximum pace and is easier to control than one hit near the rim.

TOPSPIN A rotary motion imparted to the ball by stroking up and over it. The same as an overspin.

TWIST A serve hit with a combination of topspin and sidespin, which gives the ball a kicking action off the ground.

VOLLEY Any stroke hit on the fly, before it bounces.

WESTERN GRIP An outmoded manner of holding the racket, awkward for returning low shots.